CLASSIC BREADS

Delicious
Recipes from
Around the
World

Manuela Caldirola
Nicoletta Negri
Nathalie Aru

STERLING PUBLISHING CO., INC.

New York

Photographs by Alberto Bertoldi and Walter Cadei

Library of Congress Cataloging-in-Publication Data

Caldirola, Manuela.
[Pane fatto in casa da tutto il mondo. English]
Classic breads : delicious recipes from around the world / Manuela
Caldirola, Nicoletta Negri, and Nathalie Aru.
    p. cm.
Translation of: Pane fatto in casa da tutto il mondo.
Includes index.
 ISBN 1-4027-0518-2
 1. Bread. 2. Cookery, International. I. Negri, Nicoletta. II. Aru, Nathalie. III. Title.
 TX769.C2213 2003
 641.8´15—dc21

                          2003008842

10 9 8 7 6 5 4 3 2 1

Published by Sterling Publishing Co., Inc.
387 Park Avenue South, New York, NY 10016
Originally published and copyright © in 1999 in Italy by RCS Libri S.p.A., Milan
under the title *Pane fatto in casa da tutto il mondo*
English translation by Maria Sabatino
© 2004 by Sterling Publishing Co., Inc.
Distributed in Canada by Sterling Publishing
c/o Canadian Manda Group, One Atlantic Avenue, Suite 105
Toronto, Ontario, Canada M6K 3E7
Distributed in Great Britain by Chrysalis Books
66 Brewery Road, London N7 9NT, England
Distributed in Australia by Capricorn Link (Australia) Pty. Ltd.
P.O. Box 704, Windsor, NSW 2756, Australia

Sterling ISBN 1-4027-0518-2

Preface

On the table, homemade bread gets more applause than a fancy dessert and is liked by everyone. It is almost impossible to go wrong when it comes to homemade bread. If it is made with your own hands, success and satisfaction are guaranteed. In these pages, you will find a selection of recipes for breads from around the world that you can make in your own kitchen. Some are well-known classics you may have always wondered how to bake, and some are less well-known.

You'll find focaccia and crunchy breadsticks from Italy, a traditional French baguette and pain de campagne, as well as dried pear and fig bread and multi-grain bread from Germany. Irish soda bread and

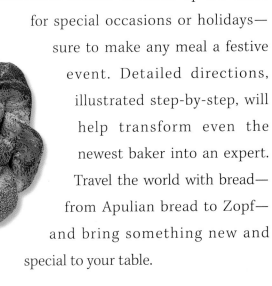

classic English scones will be welcome guests at your table. Liven up your menu with tortillas from Mexico or easy-to-prepare chapati, paratha, and naan from India. You'll find recipes for pretzels, bagels, pita, and bread baked in a garden pot from Wales.

There are even recipes and details for making decorative breads to dress up the table for special occasions or holidays—sure to make any meal a festive event. Detailed directions, illustrated step-by-step, will help transform even the newest baker into an expert. Travel the world with bread—from Apulian bread to Zopf—and bring something new and special to your table.

Contents

Decorative breads 103

Introduction

Bread is thousands of years old and it wears its age well. Over the centuries, it has evolved as it has spread throughout the world. From the beginning of time, bread has been a simple and indispensable food that has brought people together. Crunchy, tasty, and aromatic, bread is widely seen as a symbol of peace, prosperity, and harmony.

From France to India, from Mexico to Italy, we have gone around the world and united our forces in order to present to you an accurate selection of the best traditional bread recipes for lunch, dinner, or a snack in the garden. After many afternoons spent mixing and kneading dough and doing tests to ensure the best results even at home with a simple oven, we can finally reveal the secrets for making breads that are both delicious and beautiful. Delighting everyone with homemade bread is quicker and easier than you might think. By following our advice, you will discover that very little time is needed to prepare braided breads, loaves, and buns. You don't need to be an expert in the kitchen: even beginners will have very good results. Once you acquire the basic skills, you will be able to follow your fancy and prepare decorative breads. In the final section of the book, you will find exquisitely decorated centerpieces of bread dough: braided initials to use as place-markers, hearts for napkin-rings, baskets for salad bowls, suns with flaming rays, sheaves of wheat, cute country cats and mice, and braided trays to present cold cuts in an original way.

How to make bread

Equipment

Bread bricks

These are heated in the oven and used for keeping the bread hot. Wrapped in a dishcloth and put underneath the bowl with the bread dough, they help the dough to rise.

Molds, pots, and bowls

You may use steel, nonstick aluminum, Pyrex, ovenproof ceramic or terracotta molds and pots with beautiful and imaginative shapes to make bread in the form of hearts or bread with fluted borders. Bowls must be large and preferably glass or porcelain.

Oven thermometer

Placed inside the oven, it registers the temperature of the oven with precision. You can find them in kitchen stores, hardware stores, and supermarkets. Inexpensive and very useful.

Baking sheets

The best ones are nonstick. You can also use parchment paper to line a pan. To clean baking sheets, soak for 30 minutes in hot, soapy water; then remove stains and residue without scratching the pans, using a sponge and wooden dough cutter.

Molds and baking pans for muffins

For making English muffins or fantans.

Dishcloths

Made of linen or cotton, dishcloths are used to protect the shape of the bread while it rises.

Pastry brushes

Essential for glazing or finishing the surface of the bread. Use nylon brushes on raw dough and brushes with natural bristles on baked breads.

Plastic wrap and parchment paper

Use these to cover bowls while dough is rising and to protect baking pans during baking.

Timer

A timer lets us keep track of rising and baking times.

Knives, blades, and scissors

To slash the surface of the bread before or after rising, or just before the bread is put in the oven. The cuts can transform the bread into an inviting work of art.

Dough cutters

Practical and functional for mixing dough by hand and for cutting dough into pieces. Also useful for cleaning the work surface.

Scale and measuring cups/spoons

Accurate measurement of ingredients is necessary for success. Measurements are given here in 2 ways: by volume (U. S. cups, ounces, teaspoons, and tablespoons, or mL), and by weight (grams); see table on page 14.

Ingredients

White flour

This classic wheat flour, rich in starch, protein, and other substances, can be of various types depending on what kind of wheat is used and how it was milled. Bread or baking flour forms a hard dough that can be used in a bakery. In the family of wheat flours, there are so-called "hard" or "strong" flours and the "soft" or "weak" flours: the difference is in the quantity of protein that each contains. Hard wheat flours have up to 13% protein, while a soft flour rarely has over 10%. For European-style breads, the high-protein type of bread flour available in the U.S. is not suitable and therefore all-purpose flour, a blend of hard and soft wheat, is better, and is used for a wide range of baked goods.

Whole wheat flour

Uses the outer and inner parts of the wheat kernel. Usually whole wheat flour is mixed with other flours to make the bread softer.

Rye flour

This is the most finely ground product that can be made from grinding rye grains. Rye flour gives bread a dark color. The more rye flour the dough contains, the darker the color.

Whole rye flour

The product of the initial milling of the rye grains. It gives the bread an unmistakable rustic appearance. Important: don't use too much.

Corn flour

Made by finely grinding corn. Corn flour stays yellow even after baking.

Multi-grain flour

You can find this type of flour in health food or organic food stores. It is made of a mix of flours, which are more or less refined. At times, this type of flour may contain whole grains, which give the bread a country-style appearance.

Bran flour

Bran flour is obtained from the outer layer of wheat or oats. Bran flour makes the dough tasty and very soft. It is rich in fiber.

Yeast

Discovered by chance during floods in ancient Egypt, this is the leavening agent par excellence. Once it comes in contact with flour, the billions of microorganisms that make up the yeast begin to nourish themselves, multiplying and producing carbon dioxide. It is important to use the exact amount of yeast indicated in each recipe; it is an error to think that doubling the quantity of yeast will cut the rising time in half. There are three types of yeast used in breadmaking: fresh yeast, sold in cakes, which should be kept in the refrigerator; dry yeast, sold in small packets, which will keep for months, until activated with water and sugar; and natural yeast (yeast starter), a mixture of flour, water, sugar, and yeast, which can be made at home (see page 28) or purchased from a bakery.

Eggs

Eggs are always found in the richest doughs and add an unmistakable color and taste. Eggs should be used at room temperature.

Milk, cream

Taste and softness are the characteristics of milk- or cream-based dough. They are used primarily in preparing sweet or semisweet breads. Milk and cream should be used lukewarm.

Buttermilk

This is the leftover liquid that is obtained in the process of making butter from cream. It is thinner than commercial buttermilk. You can replace buttermilk with a mixture made of 8½ ounces (250 mL) of fresh milk plus one teaspoon (5 mL) of lemon juice.

Butter, oil, and other fats

These are generally used to add flavor to the dough. Oil is also used to grease the bread dough to prevent it from drying and forming a crust before baking that would need to be removed.

Water

Some bakeries advise using mineral water or water that has been boiled rather than tap water. Water should be lukewarm, not hot.

U.S. LIQUID MEASURE VOLUME-TO-VOLUME CONVERSIONS		U.S. LIQUID MEASURE TO METRIC VOLUME CONVERSIONS
¼ cup = 2 ounces	½ teaspoon = .08 ounce	
⅓ cup = 2.6 ounces	1 teaspoon = .16 ounce	
½ cup = 4 ounces	2 teaspoons = ⅓ ounce	1 teaspoon = 5 mL
⅔ cup = 5.2 ounces	3 teaspoons = ½ ounce	1 ounce = 30 mL
¾ cup = 6 ounces	6 teaspoons = 1 ounce	1 cup = 240 mL
1 cup = 8 ounces	1 tablespoon = 3 teaspoons	
	2 tablespoons = 1 ounce	
	16 tablespoons = 1 cup	

Herbs, spices, and dried fruit

These give the bread a pleasant aroma and taste. Add them before the dough is left to rise or after the first rising.

Salt

Whether fine or coarse, salt is crucial to the flavor of bread. One exception is Tuscan bread. Unlike honey, malt extract, or sugar, the salt should not come in contact with the yeast during the initial phase of mixing. In order to remember this important point, many people make a small well for the salt in the outside portion of the mound of flour and add the salt only at the last minute.

Honey and sugar

These aid in rising by feeding the yeast and give an additional touch of flavor.

Malt extract

Malt is a sprouted grain such as barley that is ground into a powder and made into an extract used in baking and brewing. Malt extract aids in rising and gives the bread a classic golden color.

Baking soda and baking powder

Both of these make the bread soft and light. Can be used alone or together. Both release carbon dioxide to make bread rise. Many recipes call for the use of baking powder, a mixture of baking soda, cream of tartar, ammonium carbonate, and vanilla in powder form. Baking powder must be sifted with the flour, and once dough prepared with baking powder is ready, it must be baked immediately.

Kneading

Kneading dough by hand is a skill that anyone can learn. The simple kneading movements become second nature and are indispensable for getting dough which is well-blended, elastic, and easy to shape. Begin by sifting the flour onto the work surface. Make a well in the flour and set out your ingredients nearby in a spiral in the following order: sugar, malt extract or honey, eggs, fats (oils, butter, lard), and finally salt (which gets added to the dough last and therefore is placed in the far corner). Salt is added last even when mixing dough with a mixer/food processor, because if it comes into direct contact with the yeast, it compromises the rising. Dissolve the yeast in the liquid indicated in the recipe; the most common liquids are water and milk. Steadily pour this mixture into the center of a well you made in the flour and begin mixing the ingredients together with the tips of your fingers. Little by little, work the dough into a ball and knead vigorously until the mixture is well-blended and elastic. To ensure that the dough has a good consistency, it should be kneaded for about 15 minutes. The ideal room temperature for mixing and kneading dough is around 80°F (25°C).

Folding the dough

This particular way to knead the dough is the secret to homemade bread. The dough is folded over onto itself but not pulled, as shown in the photo opposite. Take the dough and with closed fingers and crossed thumbs push down with the palms of your hands. Shaped into a ball like this, with three or four turns, the bread will fold over onto itself, and it will become an oval with a fold or crease down the middle. Repeat the same action many times, remembering that the dough must be turned 90 degrees before it is folded over onto itself. The crease in the dough should always be kept facing up. Patience and strength are the two most important ingredients for successful kneading; the more you knead the dough, the more the gluten will develop and the softer and better leavened the bread will be.

"Beating" the dough

According to the experts, in order to prepare the dough for some breads— e.g., panettone gastronomico—more than kneading is necessary. Once the dough is ready, it is "beaten." Beating the dough means driving in five fingers as if the dough were a bowling ball and then slamming it down on the work surface several times (see center and bottom photos).

Note about the liquids

You may need to adjust the quantity of liquid indicated for the dough. Sometimes flour that has just been ground contains more moisture and requires less water or milk. Conversely, flour that is several months old has dried up and will absorb more liquid. Remember that the dough must always be moist and never sticky. The liquid must not be too hot or it will inhibit the action of the yeast.

Raising the dough

Raising the dough is one of the most delicate phases in the preparation of bread, so it is good to carefully follow the rising times indicated and keep the room temperature at 75° to 85°F (24° to 30°C). For rising, you can use the oven, heating it on low or with warm oven bricks underneath the dough bowls. Doughs prepared with baking powder need to be put into the oven immediately after mixing. If you use fresh or dried yeast, rising is a necessary step. It can vary in length. For direct mixing, the dough must rise once or twice before being put into the oven.

Direct mixing

Dissolve the yeast, either fresh or dry, in the liquid and mix it with the other ingredients. Shape the dough into a ball, place it carefully in a bowl greased with oil, and turn the ball of dough several times to be sure it is uniformly coated with oil. Then cover the bowl with plastic wrap or dampened parchment paper.

Mixing in steps

This technique requires a yeast starter made from water, flour, and yeast, which sits for 24 hours. You can then add the other ingredients and proceed to a second rising, following the directions in the recipe. See page 28 for yeast starter recipe.

Note on rising times

Rising times vary from recipe to recipe. Usually, the dough must double in size. If you put the dough in a bread mold to rise, it must not go over the edge of the mold. Grease baking sheets and molds or use parchment paper so that you will be able to remove the bread easily.

Shaping

Round and oval breads

Round bread: Give the raised dough two folds; then turn it face-down so that the crease is touching the work surface. Turn the dough in on itself, always turning it in the same direction; use the left hand to exert steady pressure on the work surface and the right hand to shape. Oval bread: proceed in the same way, letting the dough slide forwards and backwards on the work surface while pressing it with the palms of the hands.

Long loaf

Roll out the dough with a rolling pin and roll the dough up on itself. With each turn, pinch the dough, otherwise it will unroll during baking. In order to avoid this, turn the loaf over so that the seam of the last roll comes in contact with the baking pan.

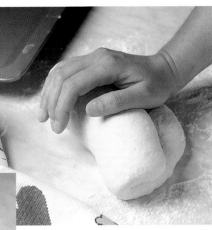

Ring-shaped bread

Shape the dough into a ball; then make a small cut in the center with the tip of a knife. Put your fingertips into the cut and with decisive but delicate movements begin to widen the hole until you obtain the desired diameter.

Rectangular loaf

Roll out the dough with a rolling pin so it is about ¾ inch (2 cm) thick. Fold the sides under and carefully place the dough into the bread mold.

Finishing touches

Milk, honey, flour...

Eggs and oil are essential to give the bread an inviting appearance. As a finishing touch or glaze, brush the surface of the bread with these ingredients. Afterwards, some spices like cumin, sesame, or poppy seeds can be sprinkled on. This can be done either before rising or during the final rising. The simplest breads are instead finished with a layer of flour, which is sifted onto the dishcloth under which the dough is left to rise.

Expert cuts

At one time, when everyone in a village baked bread in one oven, each family slashed the crust of the bread with a unique design. This way, when the baking was done it was impossible to return home with someone else's loaf. You can also create simple designs on the crusts of your breads. How? It's easy. Just slash the surface of the dough with a knife, blade, or the tip of scissors. The designs can be made either before or after the bread rises, according to the recipe.

Baking secrets

The ideal temperature for baking bread should not exceed 425°F (220°C). Either an electric or gas oven is fine as long as you know your own oven. If it gets too hot in the upper part, for example, remember to cover the surface of the bread halfway through baking with aluminum foil. If the oven gets too hot in the bottom part, put the bread onto a higher rack.

Oven thermometer

It is important to measure the actual temperature inside the oven: do not trust the oven dial. Get an oven thermometer. Follow the directions in the recipe and remember to put the bread in only after the oven is hot.

Pan of water

When you turn the oven on, put a small casserole dish containing 1½ inches (4 cm) of water in the bottom of the oven. As the water evaporates, it will create some moisture, which will prevent the crust from becoming too dry and will keep the inside of the bread soft.

Oven racks

If you look carefully at the bottom of a round or long loaf of bread, you will often notice hundreds of small holes. Bakers place the bread on oven racks riddled with small holes to ensure uniform baking. You can do the same at home: get baking sheets with holes or else, halfway through the baking, when the bread has taken on a certain shape, remove it from the baking sheet and transfer it directly to the oven rack.

Recipes

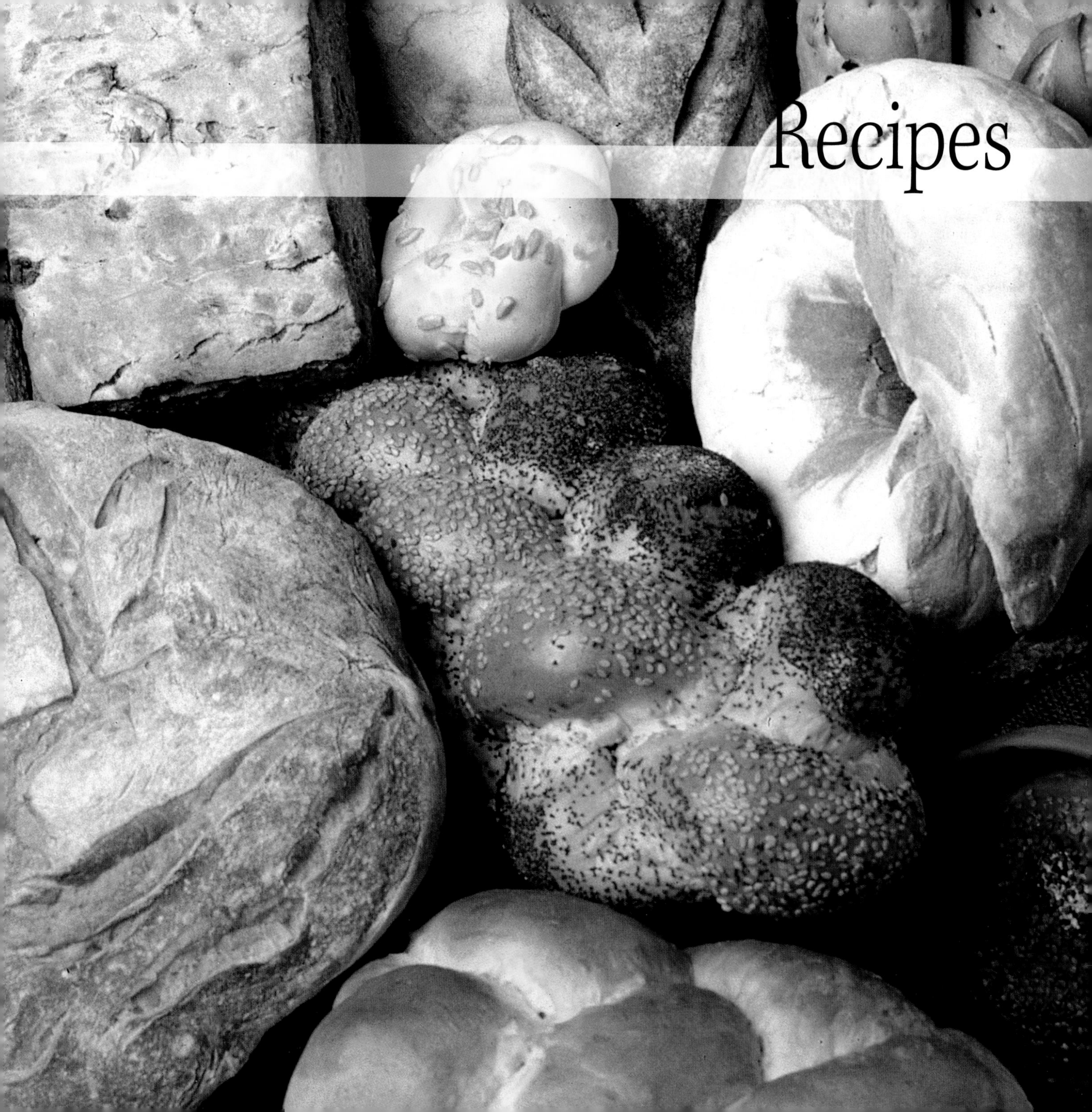

Ingredients for 4 baguettes:

2 tsp (10 g) active dry yeast

1 Tbsp (15 g) sugar or ½ Tbsp (10 g) malt extract

2 cups + 2 Tbsp (500 mL) lukewarm water (about 140°F or 60°C)

3½ cups (400 g) bread flour

2½ tsp (15 g) salt

3⅓ cups (400 g) all-purpose flour

durum wheat flour for flouring

extra-virgin olive oil

For the glaze:

1 egg white

1 Tbsp (15 mL) water

pinch of salt

Baguette France

Preparation time: 20 minutes, plus 7 hours in total for rising. *Baking time:* 25 minutes.

1. In a small bowl, dissolve the yeast and the sugar in the water and let sit for 10 minutes until creamy. Set aside. Sift 18⅓ oz (260 g) of bread flour into a large bowl and then add the salt. Make a well in the center of the flour and add the yeast mixture, mixing with a wooden spoon until well-blended. Gradually add the rest of the bread flour and all of the all-purpose flour. Cover the dough with a damp cloth and let it rise for 4 hours at room temperature. Transfer the dough to a work surface which has been lightly dusted with durum wheat flour and knead for 10 minutes.

2. Slam down the dough onto the work surface several times (see page 17). Put two tablespoons of oil in a bowl and turn the dough around in the bowl to uniformly coat it with oil. Cover with a damp cloth and let rise for 2 hours: the dough must triple in size. Punch the dough down with a closed fist, divide it into 4 parts, and form 4 long logs. Put the dough logs between the folds of a dishcloth floured with durum wheat flour, cover with a damp cloth, and let rise for one hour.

3. Prepare the egg-wash glaze by mixing together the egg white, salt, and water. Transfer the logs of dough to a baking sheet greased with oil, making sure they are not too close together. With the knife, make several slanted cuts on the surface of the dough and brush on the egg wash. Put a handful of ice cubes on the floor of the oven. Bake at 425°F (220°C) for 25 minutes.

Ingredients for 1 loaf pan 4 x 12 x 4 in (10 x 30 x 10 cm) or 2 small loaf pans:

3¾ cups (450 g) all-purpose flour

½ tsp (3 g) salt

1½ Tbsp (20 g) fresh yeast or 2¼ tsp (6 g) dry yeast

½ tsp (3 g) malt extract

8½ oz (250 mL) luke-warm milk

1½ oz (40 g) butter, melted

extra-virgin olive oil

Rectangular loaf France

This is an ideal bread for making sandwiches and canapés.

Preparation time: 30 minutes, plus 4 to 5 hours for rising. *Baking time:* 40 minutes.

1. Sift the flour and salt together onto the work surface and make a well in the center of the mixture. Put the crumbled yeast and malt extract into the center of the well. Add the milk a little at a time, mixing gently to dissolve the yeast. Begin to mix the dough, adding the flour gradually and then finally adding the melted butter. Knead and "beat" the dough (see page 17) for about 15 minutes, until the dough is well-blended and firm.

2. Form a ball with the dough and grease it uniformly with oil. Let it rise for 3 hours in a bowl covered with plastic wrap. Punch the dough down and let it rise another hour. Transfer it to a flour-covered work surface, shape it into a ball, and let rest for 5 minutes.

3. Put the dough into a well-buttered loaf pan. Cover with greased plastic wrap and let rise until it reaches ¾ of the height of the pan. Butter the lid and cover the pan.

4. Preheat oven to 425°F (220°C). Bake for 20 minutes. Then remove the cover and continue baking for another 20 minutes. If the crust becomes too hard or gets too dark, cover with aluminum foil. After it is baked, remove the bread from the pan, turn it onto a clean dishcloth, and let cool.

Ingredients for a loaf for 6 to 8 people:

For the yeast starter:

2 cups + 4 tsp (250 g) all-purpose flour

10 oz (300 mL) luke-warm water

1 Tbsp (15 g) fresh yeast

For the second dough:

2 cups + 7 oz (325 g) bread flour
or 3 oz (50 g) rye flour and 2⅓ cups (275 g) white flour

6 oz (180 mL) luke-warm water

1 tsp (5 g) fresh yeast

1 tsp (7 g) malt extract

3½ tsp (20 g) salt

Pain de campagne France

This country-style bread, particularly beautiful to look at, is delicious with cured meats, cheeses, and country style dishes.

Preparation time: 30 minutes, plus 2 days and 4 hours for rising. *Baking time:* 40 minutes.

1. For the yeast starter: sift the flour into a bowl, make a well in the flour, and pour in the water in which you have dissolved the yeast. With a wooden spoon, mix until it is well-blended. Cover with a damp cloth and let rise for 2 days at room temperature, being sure to change the cloth the second day. By this time, the mixture will be foamy and will have an acidic odor. To make bread, you only need 8½ ounces (250 mL) of this mixture.

2. Put the 8½ ounces (250 mL) of starter into a clean bowl and add the ingredients for the second dough one at a time. Knead with your hands, first in the bowl and then for about 10 minutes on a lightly floured work surface. Grease the dough with oil and let it rise for 2 hours in a bowl covered with plastic wrap.

3. Punch the dough down with a closed fist. Shape into a ball, dust the surface with flour, and place it onto a floured baking sheet. Cover with a lightly dampened cloth and let rise until doubled in size.

4. Make a series of slashes on the surface of the bread and dust once again with a small amount of flour. Bake at 425°F (220°C) for 15 minutes; then lower the temperature to 375°F (190°C) and bake for another 25 minutes. Cool the bread on a rack.

5 cups (600 g) all-purpose flour

5 tsp (20 g) sugar

1 Tbsp (15 g) fresh yeast

10 oz + 1½ tsp (300 mL) warm water

5 tsp (25 mL) extra-virgin olive oil

5 tsp (25 mL) orange blossom water

1 tsp (5 g) salt

1 Tbsp (10 g) aniseed (optional)

white flour for dusting

Fougasse France

The sweet version of this bread is the highlight of a series of 13 desserts representing Jesus and the 12 apostles, which are served on Christmas Eve.

Preparation time: 30 minutes, plus 2 hours for rising. *Baking time:* 30 minutes.

1. In a bowl, sift the flour, add half the sugar, and make a well in the center. Crumble the yeast into a small bowl, add the remaining sugar, and dilute the mixture with 7 ounces (200 mL) of lukewarm water. Pour the liquid mixture onto the flour and mix and knead the dough quickly. Note: in this phase, do not add all of the flour but only as much as necessary to obtain a creamy, well-blended mixture. Cover the bowl with plastic wrap and let rise for 30 minutes.

2. Add the remaining water, oil, orange blossom water, and salt. Begin to mix/knead the dough in the bowl; then transfer the dough onto the work surface. When the dough begins to take shape, add the aniseed and continue kneading until the dough is smooth and elastic. Oil the dough well all over and let it rise for about an hour in a bowl covered with a damp dishcloth.

3. Divide the dough into 4 to 7 parts, shape them with your hands into long rolls, and then flatten them out with a rolling pin to give them an oval shape.

4. Place the fougasses, with plenty of distance between them, on a baking pan greased with oil. With a sharp knife or the tip of scissors, make a series of alternating, symmetrical slashes and then widen them with your fingers. Lightly brush the loaves with oil and dust with a little white flour. Cover with a damp cloth and let rise just over half an hour or until doubled in size. Every so often, check that the cuts have not closed up. Bake at 390°F (200°C) for about 20 minutes and let cool on a wire rack.

Ingredients for one large rectangular loaf:

3½ Tbsp (50 g) butter

2 Tbsp (30 g) fresh yeast

¾ tsp (5 g) malt extract or sugar

6⅔ oz (200 mL) fresh lukewarm milk

2 cups + 7 oz (350 g) all-purpose flour

¾ cup (100 g) whole wheat flour

3⅓ oz (50 g) rye flour

2½ tsp (15 g) salt

2 tsp (5 g) chopped parsley

2 tsp (5 g) basil

2 tsp (5 g) chives

4 tsp (10 g) lavender flowers

2 tsp (5 g) ground cumin

extra-virgin olive oil

chopped hazelnuts and almonds (optional)

Provençal bread France

This excellent bread goes well with country-style dishes and cured meats.

Preparation time: 30 minutes, plus 1 hour for rising. *Baking time:* 30 to 35 minutes.

1. Melt butter over low heat. Dissolve the yeast and malt extract in the milk and let it activate for a few minutes. In the meantime, sift the three flours together onto the work surface. Make a well in center of the flour, pour the milk and yeast mixture into the well, and then add the melted butter, which should be just cooled to room temperature.

2. Begin to mix the dough. Gradually, as the dough starts to come together, add the salt, the chopped parsley, the herbs, the cumin, and lavender flowers. Knead the dough until it is soft, smooth, and elastic. Grease it with oil and let it rise for 25 to 30 minutes in a bowl covered with a lightly dampened cloth. If you wish, make the bread richer by adding chopped almonds and hazelnuts to the dough. Punch down the dough with a closed fist and let it rise again for half an hour.

3. Turn the dough out onto the work surface, which has been lightly floured. Grease it with oil and let it rise for another 20 minutes. With a dough cutter, cut the dough into the shape of a rectangular block. Grease the dough again and cover it, letting it rise for about 10 minutes. Use the scraps to make smaller loaves.

4. Bake for 15 minutes at 425°F (220°C); then lower the temperature to 390°F (200°C) and continue baking for another 15 to 20 minutes. For a crunchy crust, remember to put a small bowl of water in the bottom of the oven before baking the bread.

Ingredients for 1 loaf for 6 to 8 people:

6 cups + 1 oz (710 g) all-purpose flour

about 1 cup + 7 oz (450 mL) lukewarm water

1 Tbsp (12 g) fresh yeast

2½ oz (80 g) yeast starter (optional)*

extra-virgin olive oil

*See page 28 for recipe for yeast starter.

Tuscan bread Italy

This bread is notable because of its absence of salt and its simple ingredients.

Preparation time: 30 minutes, plus 3 days and 1 hour for rising. *Baking time:* 50 minutes.

1. First day: In a large bowl, mix 2½ cups (300 g) of all-purpose flour with 6⅔ ounces (200 mL) of water in which you have dissolved 1½ teaspoons (7 g) of fresh yeast. Cover with plastic wrap and let rise for 12 hours.

2. Second day: Remove the plastic wrap and add 2 ounces (50 mL) of water and 2½ ounces (80 g) of yeast starter to the dough. Mix and knead for a few minutes until the dough is well-blended; then gradually add 6⅔ oz (100 g) of sifted flour. Grease the dough with oil, place it in a large bowl, cover with the plastic wrap, and let rest for 24 hours.

3. Third day: Dissolve 1 teaspoon (5 g) of fresh yeast in 5 to 7 ounces (150 to 200 mL) of water. In the meantime, remove the plastic wrap from the bowl that the dough is in. Sift 2 cups + 4 teaspoons (250 g) of flour onto the work surface and make a well in the center. Pour water with yeast into the center of the well and add the previously made dough, broken into little pieces. Mix and knead all ingredients well, gradually adding the rest of the flour.

4. Sift 5 to 7 tablespoons (35 to 55 g) of flour onto a piece of parchment paper. Give the dough two turns, shaping it into either an oval or a round loaf. Place it on a baking sheet lined with well-floured parchment paper. Cover with a dishcloth and let rise for 1½ hours.

5. Gently remove the loaf from the parchment paper and bake at 425°F (220°C) for the first 10 minutes; then lower the temperature to 355° to 375°F (180 to 190°C) and continue baking for another 40 minutes. When the crust of the bread becomes hard, remove from the baking sheet and transfer it to the oven rack so that the baking will be uniform.

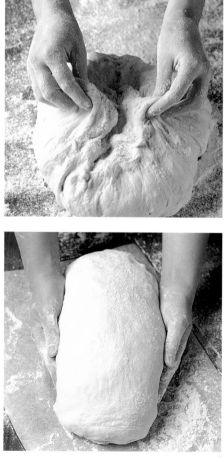

Ingredients for 1 loaf for 6 to 8 people:

5 cups (600 g) all-purpose flour

1⅔ cups (400 mL) lukewarm water

1 Tbsp + ½ tsp (17 g) fresh yeast

1 tsp (8 g) malt extract

2½ tsp (15 g) salt

extra-virgin olive oil

durum wheat flour (for flouring)

Apulian bread Italy

There is no substitute for *bruschetta*, toasted garlic bread. Scented with a clove of garlic and flavored with a dash of salt, it is a delicious accompaniment to fish, shellfish, and eggplant-based dishes. When carpaccio, pecorino cheese, salad, or raw vegetables with olive-oil dip are served, Apulian bread should not be missing.

Preparation time: 30 minutes, plus about 15 hours for rising. *Baking time:* 45 minutes.

1. The night before baking, in a large bowl, prepare the dough by mixing 2½ cups (300 g) of flour with 6⅔ ounces (200 mL) of water in which you have dissolved ½ teaspoon (2 g) of fresh yeast. Cover with plastic wrap and let rise overnight.

2. The next day, in the same bowl, add 2½ cups (300 g) of flour, 1 teaspoon (8 g) of malt extract, and 6⅔ ounces (200 mL) of water in which you have dissolved the remaining 1 tablespoon (15 g) of yeast. Begin to mix and knead the dough and, just before transferring the dough to the work surface, add the salt. Knead the dough until you obtain a soft and compact ball. Grease the dough with plenty of oil and let it rest in a large covered bowl until it doubles in size (approximately 40 minutes). Then punch down the dough with a closed fist. Cover the bowl again and let it rise for another 40 minutes.

3. Remove the plastic wrap, flip the bowl over, and let the dough slide out onto a piece of parchment paper which has been well-floured with durum wheat flour. Cover the dough with a dishcloth and let rise for another 40 minutes. Bake at 425°F (220°C) for 15 minutes; then lower the temperature to 355°F (180°C) and continue baking for another 25 to 30 minutes. When the surface of the bread becomes hard, remove it from the baking sheet and transfer it to the oven rack so that the baking will be uniform.

Ingredients for 2 large ciabatta loaves or 4 small ones:

First dough:

5 cups (600 g) all-purpose flour

¾ cup (250 g) luke-warm water

2 tsp (10 g) fresh yeast for 1½ hours rising, or 1 tsp (5 g) for overnight

4 tablespoons (57 g) extra-virgin olive oil

Second dough:

1 tsp (5 g) fresh yeast

¾ tsp (5 g) malt extract or 10 g sugar

2⅔ oz (80 mL) luke-warm water

2 oz (25 g) all-purpose flour

2½ tsp (15 g) salt

extra-virgin olive oil

Ciabatta Italy

Crunchy and aromatic, ciabatta goes well with all types of cured meats and, when toasted, with soups and pastas in broth. This bread should be eaten fresh as it tends to dry out in just a few hours.

Preparation time: 40 minutes, plus rising time (about 2½ hours or overnight).
Baking time: 30 to 40 minutes.

1. First dough: Sift the flour onto the work surface, dissolve the yeast in the water, and mix and knead until you have a well-blended mixture. Gently place the dough into a large bowl, pour the oil on the dough, and grease it uniformly. Cover with plastic wrap and let it rise for 1½ hours (or overnight). Remove the plastic wrap and pinch back the raised dough to create a hollow with your thumbs and index fingers.

2. Second dough: Dissolve the yeast and malt extract in the water and pour it slowly into the hollow of the first dough. Mix with your fingertips, adding the sifted flour first and then the salt. Knead until dough is very soft: grease it with olive oil and let it rest in a well-covered bowl for at least half an hour.

3. Remove the dough from the bowl and transfer it to a floured work surface. Divide it in half with a dough cutter. Gently place each of the halves on two pieces of well-floured parchment paper and then onto the baking sheets. With the help of the dough cutter, flatten out and shape the dough to give it the typical long, flat shape. Dust with flour and let rise for one hour. Bake for 10 minutes in an oven preheated to 425°F (220°C); then lower the temperature to 355°F (180°C) and continue baking for about another half-hour. Halfway through the baking, when the ciabatta loaves are sufficiently hard, remove from the baking sheet and place directly on the oven rack so that the bottom part of the loaves can bake.

Ingredients for about 20 breadsticks:

4 cups + 1⅓ oz (500 g) all-purpose flour

3½ Tbsp (50 g) extra-virgin olive oil

7 to 8½ oz (200 to 250 mL) lukewarm water

4 tsp (20 g) fresh yeast

4 tsp (15 g) sugar or 1 tsp (7 g) malt extract

3½ tsp (25 g) fine-grain salt

4 Tbsp (57 g) extra-virgin olive oil for oiling dough

sunflower, sesame, and poppy seeds

Breadsticks Italy

Homemade breadsticks are simple and very delicious. This basic recipe can be enriched with spices, herbs, and olives. The all-purpose flour can be replaced with whole wheat flour.

Preparation time: 40 minutes, plus ½ hour for rising. *Baking time:* 15 minutes.

1. Sift the flour onto the work surface, make a well in the center, and pour 3½ tablespoons (50 g) of oil and the water (in which you have dissolved the yeast) into the center of the well. Add the sugar or malt extract and begin to mix the dough until well-blended. Add the salt. Knead the dough for a long time, until it becomes soft and elastic. Pour 4 tablespoons (57 g) of extra-virgin olive oil into a large bowl, put the dough in the bowl, and turn it so that it is uniformly greased with the oil. Cover with plastic wrap and let rise for half an hour.

2. Turn the dough out onto a floured work surface. Divide it with the dough cutter, first in half, and then into about 20 small strips, which are more or less equal.

3. With your fingertips, hold a strip at each end and pull the dough gently but continuously so that the dough elongates without breaking until it doubles in length; then roll it in the sunflower seeds, sesame seeds, or poppy seeds. Repeat the same steps with the other strips of dough.

4. Gradually, as the breadsticks are ready, arrange them neatly and well-spaced on a baking sheet lined with parchment paper. Let them rise for half an hour. Bake at 425° to 465°F (220° to 240°C) for about 15 minutes.

Ingredients for 2 panettone:

4 cups + 1⅓ oz (500 g) all-purpose flour

3 Tbsp (40 g) fresh yeast or ½ oz (15 g) dry yeast

5¼ oz (200 g) luke-warm water

7 Tbsp (100 g) soft-ened butter

7 Tbsp (50 g) sugar

1½ tsp (10 g) salt

2 tablespoons (28 g) extra-virgin olive oil

1 paper mold for panettone (available at bakeries or pastry shops)

For glaze:

1 egg, lightly beaten

Filling:

cold cuts, salad, cheese, etc.

Panettone gastronomico Italy

This version of panettone is good for sandwiches.

Preparation time: 30 minutes, plus 2 hours for rising. *Baking time:* 45 minutes.

1. Sift the flour onto the work surface and make a well in the center. In the middle of the well, add the crumbled yeast and dissolve it in a little water. Mix with your fingertips, incorporating the flour first and then gradually the butter, sugar, and salt. Remember that the salt and fats must not come into direct contact with the yeast too soon, as they will inhibit the rising. Knead the dough for at least 15 minutes, "beating" it vigorously (see page 17). The dough will be a bit sticky; use the dough cutter to help and every so often flour your hands.

2. Pour two tablespoons (28 g) of oil into a large bowl and turn the dough around in the bowl to grease it uniformly. Cover with a dampened sheet of parchment paper and a dishcloth. Let it rise for one hour. Take the dough out and, without kneading it, shape it into a ball and place it in the paper mold. Level the dough gently with your hands. Let it rise until it reaches the edge of the paper mold. Brush with the lightly beaten egg and bake at 355°F (180°C) for 45 minutes. If the top gets dark too quickly, cover with aluminum foil and stop the baking. Let it cool on a wire rack.

3. The filling: cut off the top portion and set aside. Beginning at the bottom, cut a series of circles, ¼ inch (5 mm) thick. You need an even number to fill them two by two, like sandwiches. Reassemble, adding the filling. With a sharp knife, cut the panettone into quarters so that you end up with many slices. Reposition the top, wrap the panettone in plastic wrap, and keep in the refrigerator until ready to serve.

Ingredients for 1 loaf for 6 people:

5 tsp (25 g) fresh yeast

8½ oz (250 mL) luke-warm milk

5 cups + 3⅓ oz (650 g) all-purpose flour

¾ tsp (5 g) malt extract

7½ oz (60 g) lard

2½ tsp (15 g) salt

extra-virgin olive oil

butter

For the glaze:

1 egg, beaten

Milk bread Italy

This dough lends itself to being formed into many different shapes. The most spectacular is the braid, which you can make with up to 5 strands.

Preparation time: 30 minutes, plus 1½ hours for rising. *Baking time:* 40 minutes.

1. In a small bowl, crumble the yeast and dissolve it in lukewarm milk. Sift the flour onto the work surface and make a well in the center. In the middle of the well, add the malt extract and steadily pour in the milk mixture as you gradually incorporate all the flour. Add the lard, then the salt, and knead for about 10 minutes. Shape into a ball, grease with oil, and let it rise for about 1½ hours in a bowl covered with plastic wrap.

2. Turn the dough out onto the work surface which has been lightly floured, divide into 3 to 5 sections, and shape into strands by rolling the dough between the palms of your hands.

3. Join the ends of the strands and begin to place them one over the other in the form of a braid. Place the braid into a well-buttered loaf pan, brush the surface with the beaten egg, and let rise for 30 to 40 minutes.

4. Bake at 375°F (190°C) for 15 minutes. Then lower the temperature to 365°F (185°C) and continue baking for another 25 minutes. Remove the braid from the baking sheet and place it on a wire rack to cool.

Ingredients for one baking sheet for 4 people:

4 cups + 1⅓ oz (500 g) all-purpose flour

8½ to 9½ oz (250 to 275 mL) lukewarm water

2½ Tbsp (35 g) extra-virgin olive oil

2 tsp (10 g) fresh yeast

3½ tsp (20 g) salt

1 Tbsp (15 mL) rosemary or sage (optional)

For the glaze:

2 Tbsp (28 g) extra-virgin olive oil

6 Tbsp (90 mL) hot water

½ tsp (3 g) salt

For the toppings (optional):

2 oz (60 g) pitted olives

1 white onion

butter

olive oil

Genoan focaccia Italy

Typical of Liguria, here it is with all of its variations, exquisite and easy to prepare.

Preparation time: 30 minutes, plus 1 hour for rising. *Baking time:* 25 to 30 minutes.

1. Sift the flour onto the work surface, make a well in the center, and pour in the oil and the water in which you have dissolved the yeast. Incorporate the flour, mixing the dough with your fingertips, and only at this point add the salt. Add rosemary or sage if you wish. Knead and beat vigorously until you have a nice dough. Uniformly grease the dough with oil and let rise for 30 minutes in a bowl covered with a damp dishcloth. Turn the dough out directly onto a greased baking sheet and stretch it out with the palms of your hands. Brush the surface with oil and let rise for 20 minutes. Prepare toppings if you wish. See below.*

2. In the meantime, prepare the glaze. Mix the ingredients together in a small bowl. Brush the surface of the dough with the glaze and let rise for about one hour or until the dough has doubled in thickness. Press your fingertips over the surface of the well-risen dough so that large hollows are formed. Add toppings now if you wish.

3. Bake at 425°F (200°C) for 25 to 30 minutes. If you would like a light-colored focaccia, pour a small amount of water on the surface right before putting the dough in the oven. As soon as the focaccia comes out of the oven, brush it well with the remaining glaze.

*Toppings: Shortly before putting the dough into the oven, press 2 ounces (60 g) of pitted olives, or a white onion, sliced and sautéed for 5 minutes in butter and extra-virgin olive oil, into the dough.

Ingredients for 15 rolls:

4 cups + 3 oz (500 g) bread flour

5 tsp (25 g) fresh yeast

8½ oz (250 mL) luke-warm water

¾ tsp (5 g) malt extract

10½ Tbsp (150 g) extra-virgin olive oil

1⅔ tsp (10 g) salt

To finish (optional):

4 Tbsp (56 g) extra-virgin olive oil

6 oz (180 mL) hot water

1 tsp (5 g) salt

sesame, poppy, and cumin seeds

Olive oil bread Italy

These soft, flavorful rolls are the ideal accompaniment to antipastos and main dishes.

Preparation time: 30 minutes, plus 1½ hours for rising. *Baking time:* 25 minutes.

1. Sift the flour onto the work surface and make a well in the center. Crumble the yeast into the center of the well, dissolve it in the water, and add the malt extract. With your fingertips, begin to mix, incorporating the flour. Add 7½ tablespoons (105 g) of oil and the salt, and knead until you obtain a soft, compact, and elastic dough.

2. Pour 3 tablespoons (42 g) of oil into a large bowl, place the dough in the bowl, and turn it so that it is uniformly covered with the oil. Cover the bowl with plastic wrap and let it rise for 40 minutes.

3. Turn the dough out onto the work surface and, with a dough cutter, divide it into 20 equal sections. Shape into small logs.

4. For the small crowns: take two small logs, twist them, and join the ends together.

5. For the snail: wrap a log of dough around itself.

6. For the braid: with two fingers hold one log of dough in the center and twist the ends around each other.

7. If desired, finish with oil and seeds. See Variations below.* Place the rolls, well-spaced, on a baking sheet, and let them rise for 45 minutes. Bake in an oven preheated to 390°F (200°C) for 25 minutes.

*Variations: Before baking, brush the surface with a mixture of 4 tablespoons (56 g) of olive oil beaten with 6 ounces (180 mL) of hot water and 1 teaspoon (5 g) of salt. Then sprinkle with sesame, poppy, and cumin seeds.

**Ingredients for 1 loaf
for 4 people:**

17 oz (500 mL) whole
milk

2 Tbsp (30 mL) lemon
juice

½ cup (30 g) bran

1⅔ tsp (10 g) fine-
grain salt

1 level tsp baking soda

2 cups + 7 oz (350 g)
all-purpose flour

7 oz (120 g) whole
wheat flour

2 Tbsp (30 g) very cold
butter, cut into small
cubes

Soda bread Ireland

The original recipe calls for buttermilk, which is produced when churning
cream to make butter; this ingredient can be replaced with whole milk and
lemon juice.

Preparation time: 20 minutes. *Baking time:* 40 minutes.

1. In a jar, mix the milk and the lemon juice and let sit for 5 minutes. In the
meantime, put the bran, the salt, the baking soda, and the sifted flours into a
large bowl. Mix well with a wooden spoon. Add the butter and begin to mix
vigorously with your fingertips. Make quick movements from the top to the
bottom, to incorporate as much air as possible during the mixing; the dough
should have a sandy consistency.

2. Gradually add in the milk and lemon juice mixture. When the dough starts
to change consistency, transfer it to a lightly floured work surface and knead
quickly until the dough is smooth.

3. Shape the dough into a flat disc, place on a floured baking sheet, and dust
with all-purpose flour. With a sharp knife, make a cross on the surface. Bake
for about 40 minutes at 425° F (220°C), until the loaf is a nice golden-brown
color. Wrap the bread in a clean dishcloth and let it cool.

Ingredients for one loaf for 4 people:

2¼ cups (300 g) white flour

1⅓ cup (150 g) bread flour

5 tsp (25 g) fresh yeast (dry yeast is not recommended)

7 oz (200 mL) luke-warm water

2 tsp (10 mL) extra-virgin olive oil

1⅓ tsp (8 g) salt

For the glaze:

1 egg, lightly beaten

Cottage loaf England

Preparation time: 30 minutes, plus about 1 hour and 20 minutes for rising.
Baking time: 40 minutes.

1. Sift the flours onto the work surface, make a well in the center, and put the crumbled yeast in the well, pouring in the lukewarm water to dissolve it. Mix the dough with the tips of your fingers, incorporating the flour a little at a time. When the dough starts to come together, add the oil and then the salt. "Beat" the dough (see page 17) until it is soft and compact. Grease it uniformly with oil and let it rise for one hour in a bowl covered with dampened plastic wrap.

2. Punch down the dough, put it back in the bowl, cover, and let rise for another 20 minutes. Turn the dough out onto the work surface and, without kneading it, divide it into two sections, one double the size of the other.

3. Grease the dough sections again and let rest for 5 minutes, covered with dampened parchment paper. Shape into two balls and gently flatten them; place the larger one on a greased baking sheet. Brush with water and place the small one on top, centering it precisely. Put index and middle fingers in the center of dough; push down towards the bottom for a minute.

4. Place the loaf on a baking sheet lined with parchment paper, brush with the lightly beaten egg, cover with another sheet of dampened parchment paper, and let it rise for 40 minutes. Brush the surface again with the beaten egg. With a sharp knife, make a series of clean cuts of a depth of ½ inch (1 cm), around the perimeters of the two flattened balls of dough.

5. Cover the bread with a large pot turned upside down (the pot must be twice the size of the dough) and bake at 390°F (200°C) for 15 minutes. Then remove the pot and leave the bread in the oven for another 15 to 25 minutes. Let cool on a wire rack.

Ingredients for one loaf for 4 to 6 people:

3½ Tbsp (50 g) butter

3½ oz (100 mL) luke-warm water

½ cup (125 mL) luke-warm milk

5 tsp (25 g) fresh yeast or 2¼ tsp (7 g) dry yeast

¾ tsp (5 g) malt extract or 2½ tsp (10 g) cane sugar

2 cups + 1 oz (300 g) whole wheat flour

1⅔ cups (200 g) all-purpose flour

2½ tsp (15 g) salt

extra-virgin olive oil

For the glaze:

1 egg white

Optional:

oat flakes

pat of butter

Whole wheat bread England

Crunchy and flavorful, this bread can accompany any meal and stays fresh for days.

Preparation time: 30 minutes, plus 1 hour and 40 minutes for rising. *Baking time:* 30 to 40 minutes.

1. Melt the butter over low heat. In the meantime, pour the water and the milk into a large bowl. Add the yeast and malt extract and mix until both are completely dissolved. Add the two sifted flours gradually, steadily pour in the melted butter, and add the salt last. Knead for 15 minutes. Grease the dough uniformly with oil, place it in a bowl, cover with a damp cloth, and let rise for 40 minutes. Punch down the dough with your fist and let rise for another 30 minutes.

2. Place the dough in a well-greased bread mold, brush the surface with the lightly beaten egg white, and let the dough rise away from drafts for 30 minutes or until it doubles in size. To serve it the original way, with salty dishes or with jam and butter, stamp the surface with a butter stamp before putting the dough in the oven. If desired, you can enrich this whole wheat bread by sprinkling on oat flakes before putting it in the oven. Bake in an oven preheated to 375°F (190°C) for 30 to 40 minutes.

3. At the moment the bread is brought to the table, place a pat of butter—shaped with the butter stamp and left in the freezer for 10 minutes to harden—in the hollow of the bread.

Ingredients for 24 muffins:

¼ cup (60 mL) melted butter

8½ oz (250 mL) scalded milk, left to cool to room temperature

8½ oz (250 mL) hot water (140 to 160°F; 60 to 70°C)

1 cup (200 g) sugar

5 tsp (25 g) fresh yeast or 2¼ tsp (7 g) dry yeast

8¾ cups (1 kg) bread flour

1 tsp (5 g) salt

extra-virgin olive oil

durum wheat flour

Muffins England

These delicious muffins are perfect for the classic tea at 5. Before serving, toast them and spread with butter and jam. They also go well with savory foods.

Preparation time: 15 minutes, plus 1½ hours for rising. *Baking time:* 15 minutes.

1. Cut the butter into small pieces, place in a small saucepan, and melt over very low heat. In the meantime, pour the milk and water into a large bowl, add the sugar and the yeast, mix, and let the ingredients dissolve.

2. Steadily pour in the lukewarm melted butter and add 3½ cups (390 g) of sifted flour. Beat the mixture with a wooden spoon for a few minutes to mix the ingredients. Then add the salt and the rest of the flour. Less than the quantity of flour indicated may be enough: you can tell by feeling the dough, which should be soft and rather sticky.

3. Knead with floured hands for 10 minutes; then grease the dough well with oil and let it rise for one hour. Punch down the dough with a closed fist, transfer it to the durum wheat-floured work surface, and knead for 5 minutes. Cover with well-greased plastic wrap and let rise for 30 minutes.

4. Hold the dough with one hand. "Strangling" it between your thumb and index finger, divide it into 24 portions and place them in the muffin pans, filling them no more than three-fourths of the way. Let rise for 30 minutes. Bake at 355°F (180°C) for 15 minutes.

Ingredients for 35 scones, 5 cm in diameter:

2 cups + 4 tsp (250 g) flour

1 tsp (4.5 g) baking soda

1 tsp (5 g) salt

1 tsp (4.5 g) cream of tartar

1 egg

5 oz (150 mL) luke-warm milk

1¾ Tbsp (25 g) butter

2½ tsp (10 g) sugar

For the glaze:

1 egg

milk

Scones England

A purely English tradition, scones spread with honey, butter, and jam are never lacking at breakfast and teatime.

Preparation time: 25 minutes. *Baking time:* 25 minutes.

1. Melt the butter over low heat. Let cool to lukewarm. Sift the flour, the baking soda, salt, and the cream of tartar together. Make a well in the center and crack an egg into the center of the well. Steadily pour in the milk and the melted butter, add the sugar, and begin to mix. Knead until you obtain a smooth, soft, and compact dough. Roll out the dough to be ¾ inch thick (2 cm).
2. With a cookie cutter 2 inches (5 cm) in diameter, cut out many circles. Brush with the remaining egg, lightly mixed with a few spoonfuls of milk, and bake in an oven preheated to 355°F (180°C) for not more than 15 minutes.

**Ingredients for
20 to 25 rolls:**

5⅔ cups (680 g) all-
purpose flour

2½ tsp (15 g) salt

4¼ Tbsp (60 g) very
cold butter, cut into
small pieces

1 Tbsp (15 g) fresh
bakery yeast or 2¼ tsp
(7 g) dry yeast

4 Tbsp sugar

1⅔ cups (400 mL)
lukewarm milk

1 egg

extra-virgin olive oil

For the glaze:

milk

1 egg, beaten

Bridge rolls England

Excellent plain or filled, sweet or salted, these little rolls are perfect as
delicious snacks to cheer up bridge parties. They are also ideal for breakfasts,
buffets, or picnics.

Preparation time: 30 minutes, plus 1½ hours for rising. *Baking time:* 15
minutes.

1. In a large bowl, sift the flour and salt together. Add the small pieces of
butter and mix with your fingertips until you have a sandy mixture. In a small
bowl, crumble the yeast and add the sugar. Pour 4 tablespoons (60 mL) of
milk over the dry ingredients and mix until well-blended. Make a well in the
center of the flour and pour in the yeast mixture. Begin to mix the dough
while you steadily pour in the remaining milk and one beaten egg. Knead the
dough for several minutes; if the dough is still sticky, add a little flour until
the dough becomes firm and elastic.

2. Grease the dough uniformly with oil and let rise for 1½ hours in a bowl
covered with plastic wrap. Turn the dough out onto the work surface and
with a dough cutter divide it into 20 to 25 small, equal-sized pieces and then
shape into oval rolls.

3. Arrange the oval rolls, well-spaced, on a buttered baking sheet. Brush with
a little oil and cover with a damp cloth. Let rise for half an hour.

4. Brush the rolls with a little milk mixed with a beaten egg and bake for 5
minutes in an oven preheated to 425°F (220ºC); then lower the temperature
to 390°F (200ºC) and continue baking for another 5 to 10 minutes. The bridge
rolls are done when they appear golden in color. Remove them from the oven,
cover with a dry cloth, and let cool.

Ingredients for 2 loaves baked in 2 tall clay pots, 5 inches (12 cm) in diameter:

extra-virgin olive oil

8½ oz (150 g) whole wheat flour

2 cups + 7 oz (350 g) all-purpose flour

1 Tbsp (15 g) fresh yeast or 1¼ tsp (4 g) dry yeast

5 oz (150 mL) luke-warm whole milk

3½ Tbsp (50 g) butter

1 bunch chives

1 sprig thyme

1 sprig basil or oregano

1 clove garlic (optional)

½ cup (120 mL) water

½ tsp (3 g) malt extract or 1¼ tsp (5 g) sugar

1⅔ tsp (10 g) salt

To finish:

1 egg

fennel and poppy seeds

Welsh clay pot loaf Wales

This is the ideal bread for picnics or for snacks in the garden. It goes best with fresh cheeses and cured meats.

Preparation time: 3 to 4 hours for preparing pots; dough preparation, 10 minutes, plus 1 hour for rising. *Baking time:* 35 to 40 minutes.

1. Before preparing the bread, it is first necessary to wash the new clay pots very well and grease them with plenty of oil. Then put the pots in a 390°F (200°C) oven for 3 to 4 hours. This procedure needs to be done only the first time that you use the pots.

2. In a large bowl, sift the two types of flour together and make a well in the center. Dissolve the yeast in the milk and pour into the center of the well. Mix quickly with your fingertips or with a small whisk without incorporating all of the flour, using only the amount necessary to create a smooth mixture. Cover with plastic wrap and let rest for 20 minutes. In the meantime, melt the butter over very low heat, combine the herbs, chives, and the peeled clove of garlic together, and chop finely.

3. Remove the plastic wrap from the bowl. Add the water, the lukewarm melted butter, the malt extract, and the chopped herbs to the dough. Knead until the dough is well-blended and then add the salt.

4. Grease the pots, arrange the dough in them, brush the dough with the beaten egg, and let rise for 30 to 40 minutes, until doubled in size. Brush the surface again with the egg, and sprinkle with the fennel and poppy seeds. Bake for 30 minutes in an oven preheated to 390°F (200°C).

Ingredients for 4 loaves:

6⅓ Tbsp (90 g) butter

8½ oz (250 mL) whole lukewarm milk

1 egg

2½ tsp (10 g) sugar

4 tsp (20 g) fresh yeast

5⅔ cups (680 g) all-purpose flour

2½ tsp (15 g) salt

extra-virgin olive oil

To finish:

2 Tbsp butter

Parker House rolls United States

This bread was created in the famous Parker House Hotel in Boston.

Preparation time: 40 minutes, plus 1½ hours for rising. Baking: 30 minutes.

1. Cut 4⅓ tablespoons (60 g) of butter into small pieces and melt over low heat. Add in 5 ounces (150 mL) of the milk, pouring steadily, and then the egg, mixing continuously with a whisk to ensure ingredients are well-blended. Remove from heat and let cool to lukewarm. In the meantime, pour 3½ ounces (100 mL) of milk into a pitcher, add the sugar and the crumbled yeast and dissolve, mixing the ingredients with a wooden spoon. Sift the flour into a large bowl, make a well in the center, and steadily pour in the milk with the dissolved yeast. Mix, incorporating a little of the flour. Next, add the mixture of milk, butter, and egg, and finally add the salt. Knead the ingredients first in the bowl and then on the work surface. Slam the dough down onto the work surface several times until it becomes soft and elastic.

2. Grease the dough uniformly with oil and place it in a bowl. Cover with a damp dishcloth and let rise for 1 hour. Transfer the dough to the work surface and roll out with a rolling pin. With a knife, cut into four strips, each 2 inches (5 cm) wide.

3. Melt about 2 tablespoons (30 g) of butter, brush it on the dough strips, and fold them into a fan shape. Brush the surface again with the melted butter and let rise for 20 to 30 minutes, away from drafts. Repeat the same procedure with all of the strips of dough. In an oven preheated to 390°F (200°C), bake for about 30 minutes.

Ingredients for 20 bagels:

3¾ cups (450 g) all-purpose flour

1 Tbsp (15 g) fresh yeast or 2 tsp (6 g) dry yeast

6 oz (170 mL) luke-warm water

4 oz (120 mL) luke-warm milk

2 Tbsp (30 g) melted butter

1 tsp (5 g) salt

extra-virgin olive oil

1 egg beaten with 2 Tbsp (30 mL) milk

To finish (optional):

egg whites

1 Tbsp (15 mL) hot water

sesame and poppy seeds

Bagels United States

These small bread rings of European Jewish origin have become a classic of American cuisine. They are excellent hot, cold, plain or with fresh cheese.

Preparation time: 40 minutes, plus 2 hours for rising. *Baking time:* 25 minutes.

1. Sift the flour into a large bowl and make a well in the center. Put the crumbled yeast in the center of the well and add the water and milk. Mix with your fingertips to incorporate a little of the flour. Steadily pour in the melted butter, mix, and add the salt. Knead the dough to make it soft and compact. When it begins to come away from the bowl, transfer it to the work surface. Continue kneading for several minutes; then oil it all over and let rise in the bowl for 1 hour. Turn the dough out onto the work surface and divide it into 20 small portions. Shape them into balls, flatten each with the palm of your hand, make a hole in the center of each ball with your thumb, and shape them into rings. Place them, well-spaced, on several oiled baking sheets.

2. Brush with the egg beaten with milk and cover with a dry dishcloth. Let rise for one hour or until they have doubled in size. In a large, shallow pot, bring water to a boil. Lower the heat and drop the bagels in. Cook for 1 minute; then turn and cook for another 30 seconds. Drain the bagels and arrange them on a baking sheet. Bake in a 390°F (200°C) oven for 25 minutes.

3. To enrich the bagels, brush their surfaces with egg whites diluted with 1 tablespoon (15 mL) of hot water, and sprinkle with sesame and poppy seeds.

Ingredients for 8 fan-shaped rolls:

8½ oz (250 mL) luke-warm milk (85°F or 30°C) mixed with 1 Tbsp (15 mL) lemon juice*

6⅓ Tbsp (90 g) butter

5⅔ cups (680 g) all-purpose flour

1 tsp (5 g) salt

a pinch of baking soda

1 Tbsp (15 g) fresh yeast

2 Tbsp (42 g) honey

extra-virgin olive oil

*Or 3⅓ oz (100 mL) water mixed with 5 oz (150 mL) whole milk yogurt.

Fantans United States

These crunchy and crumbly rolls go well with rich and elaborate dishes.

Preparation time: 40 minutes, plus 1 hour and 30 minutes for rising. *Baking time:* 15 minutes.

1. In a bowl, pour in the milk mixed with lemon juice. Add the yeast and honey and let the mixture sit for 30 minutes. Melt 4⅓ tablespoons (60 g) of butter. In the meantime, sift the flour with the salt and baking soda into a second bowl. Make a well in the center and steadily pour in the yeast mixture. Mix well with a wooden spoon and when the dough becomes dense, add the melted butter. Knead well, first in the bowl and then on the work surface. Uniformly oil the dough and let rise for 30 minutes in a bowl covered with plastic wrap. When the dough doubles in size, punch down with your fist. Let the dough rise for another 15 minutes. Turn the dough out onto a floured work surface, and roll out with a rolling pin to ⅛ inch (3 mm) in thickness. Be careful not to tear the dough, which must be handled gently.

2. Melt the remaining butter and brush on both sides of the dough. With a sharp knife, cut the dough lengthwise into four strips, each 2½ inches (7 cm) wide. Stack the strips on top of each other and cut into 8 portions. For each portion, gently press one end together and fan out the other end; then place in a muffin pan. Let rise for 30 minutes, away from drafts. Bake for 15 minutes in an oven preheated to 425°F (220°C).

Ingredients for one loaf for 4 to 6 people:

3⅓ cups (400 g) rye flour

6⅔ oz (100 g) all-purpose flour

1¼ tsp (5 g) sugar

2 Tbsp (30 g) fresh yeast

3½ oz (100 mL) luke-warm water

12 oz (350 mL) luke-warm milk

1⅔ tsp (10 g) salt

3½ (100 g) fennel seeds

¼ cup (50 g) dried figs (optional)

⅓ cup (50 g) raisins (optional)

extra-virgin olive oil

To finish:

1 egg

pinch of salt

1⅔ oz (50 g) fennel seeds

Black bread with fennel seeds Germany

This typical Nordic bread goes well with spiced dishes, cheeses, cured meats, and smoked salmon. It will stay fresh for up to one week.

Preparation time: 30 minutes, plus 4 hours for rising. *Baking time:* 40 minutes.

1. Mix the flours and sift them onto the work surface. Make a well in the center and add the sugar and the crumbled yeast in the middle of the well. Begin to mix, steadily pouring in the water and milk. When the dough begins to come together, add the salt. Knead until the dough is soft; then flatten it with your hands and add 3½ oz (100 g) of fennel seeds to the center. Continue kneading until the seeds are uniformly distributed throughout the dough. Grease the dough with oil and let rise for 1½ hours in a bowl covered with plastic wrap.

2. Turn the dough out onto a lightly floured work surface and shape into a long loaf. If you wish, enrich the bread by adding ¼ cup (50 g) of chopped dried figs and ⅓ cup (50 g) of raisins to the dough. With a sharp knife, make several diagonal slashes on the dough (see photo). Brush the surface with oil and let rise for 2 hours and 30 minutes, away from drafts.

3. Beat the egg with a pinch of salt and very gently brush onto the surface of the dough. Then pat on 1⅔ oz (50 g) of the fennel seeds. In an oven preheated to 390°F (200°C), bake for 35 to 40 minutes. Let the bread cool on a wire rack.

Ingredients for 1 loaf for 4 to 6 people:

⅓ cup (70 g) dried pears cut into small pieces

⅓ cup (70 g) dried figs cut into small pieces

⅓ cup (70 g) pitted prunes

10¼ oz (300 mL) apple or prune juice

3⅓ cups (400 g) all-purpose flour

½ cup (60 g) rye flour

a pinch salt

7½ Tbsp (90 g) sugar

3½ tsp (18 g) fresh yeast or 2¼ tsp (7 g) dry yeast

5 oz (150 mL) luke-warm water

extra-virgin olive oil

1 grated lemon rind

1 cup (100 g) almonds and hazelnuts roughly chopped

Dried pear and fig bread Germany

This hearty, flavorful German specialty, full of delicious dried fruit, will be the highlight of your breakfast or winter snack.

Preparation time: Fruit soaking: 12 hours. Assembly, 40 minutes, plus 2 to 3 hours for rising. *Baking time:* 45 minutes.

1. In a large bowl, soak the pears, figs, and prunes with 5 ounces (150 mL) of apple or prune juice. Let them sit for 12 hours. Drain the fruit and squeeze out well.

2. In a large bowl, mix the all-purpose and rye flours, the salt, and the sugar. Make a well in the center and pour in the yeast, dissolved in the remaining fruit juice, and 5 ounces (150 mL) of lukewarm water. Mix in the flour a little at a time. The dough should be soft but not sticky; if necessary, add a little flour. Knead for about 10 minutes on a floured work surface. Place the dough in a bowl, grease the dough uniformly with oil, cover with a damp dishcloth, and let rise for 1½ hours.

3. Roll out the dough into a flat rectangle and arrange the fruit, grated lemon rind, and hazelnuts and almonds on top of the dough (see photo). Roll up the dough, turning in the ends so that the dried fruit ends up on the inside of the bread.

4. Shape into an oval loaf, place it on a baking sheet lined with parchment paper, and dust with flour. Make three lengthwise slashes on the surface of the dough. Cover with a lightly dampened cloth and let rise for about 1½ hours. Bake in an oven preheated to 355°F (180°C) for 45 minutes. Let cool on a wire rack.

Ingredients for one loaf for 4 to 6 people:

2⅔ cups (400 g) multi-grain flour

1 cup (100 g) bread flour

½ Tbsp (10 g) honey

4 tsp (20 g) fresh yeast

8½ to 9 oz (250 to 300 mL) lukewarm water

2½ tsp (15 g) salt

extra-virgin olive oil

For the glaze:

1 egg

Multi-grain bread Germany

This recipe has many varieties. The version presented here is the simplest and quickest. It makes bread that can be served with butter, honey, and jam as well as roasts, cheeses, and grilled meat.

Preparation time: 20 minutes, plus 1½ hours for rising. *Baking time:* 40 minutes.

1. Sift the flours onto the work surface. Make a well in the center and add in the honey and crumbled yeast. Steadily pour in the water and begin to mix and then knead. Do not pour in all of the water at once, since multi-grain flours are not all the same: some absorb more water than others. Regulate the amount of water by feeling the dough, which should be soft and compact but not sticky. Last, add the salt.

2. Grease the dough uniformly with oil and place it on a baking sheet. Cover with a damp cloth and let it rise for half an hour.

3. Transfer the dough to the work surface, shape the loaf, and decorate it with several slashes in the shape of a sunburst. Brush with the beaten egg and let rise in a location away from drafts for about one hour.

4. Bake in an oven preheated to 425°F (220°C) for 35 to 40 minutes. Be sure to remove the bread from the baking sheet halfway through the baking time and transfer it directly to the oven rack to ensure uniform baking.

Ingredients for 16 pretzels:

5¾ oz (170 mL) luke-warm water

4 oz (120 mL) luke-warm milk

1 Tbsp (15 g) fresh yeast or 2 tsp (6 g) dry yeast

3¾ cups (450 g) all-purpose flour

1 tsp (5 g) salt

2 Tbsp (30 g) melted butter

extra-virgin olive oil

To finish:

1 egg beaten with 2 Tbsp (30 mL) milk

coarse salt

Pretzels Germany

These soft, flavorful, salty pretzels are good for teas, buffets, and picnics.

Preparation time: 40 minutes, plus 2 hours for rising. *Baking time:* 25 minutes.

1. Pour the water and the milk into a bowl and dissolve the yeast. In another bowl, sift the flour with the salt and make a well in the center. Steadily pour the yeast mixture into the center of the well, mixing with a wooden spoon and blending in the flour. Then add the melted butter.

2. Continue to mix the dough, until it comes off the sides of the bowl. Then transfer the dough to the work surface and knead for another 5 minutes. Grease the dough uniformly with oil and let it rise for 1 hour in the bowl covered with plastic wrap.

3. Turn the dough out onto the work surface, knead for five minutes, and then divide it into 16 equal portions. Shape the portions into small balls, place them on a thick layer of flour, and cover with a cloth.

4. Take one ball and roll it into a rope 15 inches (40 cm) long with the center part thicker than the ends. With your fingertips, hold the ends, twist them, and attach them using light pressure to the area where the rope starts to thin. Arrange the pretzel rings on a buttered baking sheet and let them rest for 10 minutes—the time required to bring a large pot of salted water to a boil.

5. Once the water boils, reduce the heat and immerse the pretzels one at a time. When the pretzels float to the surface, drain them and gently place them first on a dishcloth and then on a baking sheet lined with parchment paper. Brush with the egg beaten with milk. Sprinkle with coarse salt and bake at 390°F (200°C) for 25 minutes. Let cool on a wire rack; they can be served warm or cold.

Ingredients for 1 braided loaf for 6 to 8 people:

juice of half a lemon

5 oz (150 mL) cream

5 cups (600 g) all-purpose flour

2 Tbsp (30 g) fresh yeast or 3⅓ tsp (10 g) dry yeast

5 oz (150 mL) luke-warm milk

1 egg

7¾ Tbsp (110 g) softened butter, cut in small pieces

2 tsp (12 g) salt

extra-virgin olive oil

To finish (optional):

1 egg, beaten

oat flakes

sesame and poppy seeds

Zopf Switzerland

This is a rich and flavorful bread that the Swiss love to make at home on Sunday. It is excellent with butter and jam and ideal for sandwiches as it doesn't contain sugar.

Preparation time: 30 minutes, plus 2 hours for rising. *Baking time:* 40 minutes.

1. In a bowl, mix the lemon juice with the cream and let sit for 5 minutes.

2. In the meantime, sift the flour onto the work surface, make a well in the center, and add the crumbled yeast. Steadily pour the milk and the soured cream (lemon juice and cream mixture) into the center of the well and mix with your fingertips to dissolve the yeast.

3. Add the egg, the softened butter cut into small pieces, and the salt. Mix, and then knead for about 20 minutes, slamming the dough down onto the work surface until it is soft and compact (see "Beating" the dough, p. 17).

4. Place in a bowl covered with plastic wrap and let rest for 1 hour. Transfer the dough to the work surface and, without kneading it, shape into a ball and then divide it into three parts of equal weight. Shape the three parts into thick ropes.

5. Lightly flour the work surface and lay the ropes out in front of you lengthwise. Join them at one end and then braid.

6. Finish the braid by pressing together the three ends. Place on a baking sheet lined with parchment paper. Cover with plastic wrap greased with oil and let rise for about 50 minutes. Brush with the beaten egg. You can enrich the bread by patting on oat flakes and sesame and poppy seeds after it has been brushed with egg. Bake in an oven preheated to 355°F (180°C) for 30 to 40 minutes.

Ingredients for 6 small loaves:

2 Tbsp (30 g) fresh yeast

2½ Tbsp (30 g) sugar

8½ oz (250 mL) beer

2½ cups (300 g) all-purpose flour

1⅔ cups (200 g) rye flour

1 egg

1⅔ oz (50 mL) extra-virgin olive oil

2½ tsp (15 g) salt

For the glaze:

3⅓ oz (100 mL) beer

2 oz (30 g) rye flour

1 tsp salt

Beer bread Belgium

A soft, light bread that is an ideal accompaniment to any dish.

Preparation time: 20 minutes, plus 1½ hours for rising. *Baking time:* 20 to 25 minutes.

1. Put the crumbled yeast and the sugar in a bowl. Steadily pour in the beer and mix with a wooden spoon until the mixture is well-blended.

2. In a large bowl, sift the two flours together and make a well in the center. In the center of the well, add the egg, the oil, the salt, and the yeast and beer mixture. Mix and knead well. The dough will be very sticky—if necessary add a little all-purpose flour.

3. Grease the dough with oil and let rise for half an hour in a bowl covered with plastic wrap. Then punch it down with a closed fist and continue to let it rise for another 20 minutes.

4. Turn the dough out onto a work surface floured with the rye flour and divide the dough into 6 equal parts.

5. Prepare the glaze, mixing the rye flour, the salt, and the beer in a small bowl. Shape the dough into 6 small round, flat loaves. Place on a baking sheet and brush with the glaze. Let rise away from drafts for about 30 minutes. Bake at 425°F (220°C) for 20 to 25 minutes.

Ingredients for 1 bread ring for 4 to 6 people:

1 cup + 6½ oz (220 g) rye flour

2 cups + 7 oz (350 g) all-purpose flour + extra

2 tsp (12 g) salt

2 tsp (10 g) cumin seeds

1 Tbsp (12 g) sugar

1 Tbsp (18 g) fresh yeast

5 oz (150 mL) luke-warm water

7 oz (200 mL) luke-warm milk

1 onion

2 Tbsp (28 g) olive oil

Onion bread Scandinavia

Flavorful and crunchy, this bread is a good accompaniment to antipasti and flavorful main dishes.

Preparation time: 45 minutes, plus 2½ hours for rising. *Baking time:* 45 minutes.

1. In a large bowl, add the flours, the salt, and the cumin seeds. Mix them, make a well in the center, and add the sugar and the crumbled yeast. Steadily pour in the water and milk. Mix well with your fingertips to blend in the flour. Knead vigorously.
2. Grease the dough with oil and let rise for 20 minutes in a bowl covered with a damp cloth.
3. In the meantime, finely chop the onion and lightly sauté it in 2 tablespoons (28 g) of olive oil over very low heat.
4. Turn the dough out onto the work surface, flatten, and add the room-temperature onions to the center. Knead, adding the amount of flour necessary to obtain a soft, compact dough that is not sticky. Grease the dough again with oil, place in a bowl, cover well, and let rise for one hour.
5. Flour the work surface, and turn the dough out onto it. Shape into a ring by putting your hands in the middle of the dough and delicately stretching out the center hole. Brush with a little olive oil, dust with flour, and slash the surface with one cut. Let rise for another hour.
6. Bake at 375°F (190°C) for 40 to 45 minutes; let cool on a wire rack.

Ingredients for 1 Bundt loaf, for 4 to 6 people:

2 cups (250 g) walnuts

2 cups + 1 oz (300 g) whole wheat flour

1⅔ cups (200 g) all-purpose flour

6⅔ oz (100 g) rye flour

2 Tbsp (30 g) fresh yeast

¾ tsp (5 g) malt extract

8½ oz (250 mL) luke-warm water

1¾ Tbsp (25 g) luke-warm melted butter

2½ tsp (15 g) salt

extra-virgin olive oil

Nordic bread with walnuts Norway

This nutritious, tasty bread has very ancient origins. The original recipe calls for very long rising times. This version, to be made at home, is very similar to the more elaborate traditional recipe.

Preparation time: 40 minutes, plus 1 hour for rising. *Baking time:* 45 minutes.

1. Shell the walnuts and put aside the nicest ones; roughly chop the others. Put the flours in a bowl, mix them well, and pour onto the work surface. Make a well in the center and put the crumbled yeast and malt extract into the middle of the well. Steadily pour in the water and begin to incorporate some of the flour. Add the lukewarm melted butter by spoonfuls and continue mixing, slowly adding in the salt and the roughly chopped walnuts. Knead and slam the dough down for 15 minutes. Grease the dough with oil and let rise for 40 minutes in a bowl covered with a damp dishcloth.
2. Turn the dough out onto a floured work surface, give it two turns, and shape it into a ring. Place nice walnut pieces onto the bottom of a buttered Bundt pan and add the dough ring on top.
3. Let rise for 20 minutes; then bake at 375°F (190°C) for 40 to 45 minutes. Let the bread cool before removing it from the pan.

Ingredients for one loaf for 4 to 6 people:

½ pound (200 g) boiled potatoes, grated or riced

2 Tbsp (30 g) butter

3⅔ cups (500 g) white bread flour

1½ tsp (10 g) malt extract or 2½ tsp (10 g) sugar

5 tsp (25 g) fresh yeast or 2¼ tsp (7 g) dry yeast

18⅔ oz (550 mL) luke-warm water

2½ tsp (15 g) salt

extra-virgin olive oil

Potato bread Finland

This bread's delicate flavor makes it perfect for all occasions for accompanying any dish.

Preparation time: 40 minutes, plus 1 hour and 30 minutes for rising. *Baking time:* 20 minutes.

1. Wash and peel the potatoes and then boil them. Drain them well and let cool. Then put them through a potato ricer.
2. Melt the butter in a small pan. Set aside. Sift the flour onto the work surface and make a well in the center. Add the malt extract or sugar and the crumbled yeast. Steadily pour in the water and melted butter, which should be just lukewarm, and finally the potatoes. Mix and knead carefully and then add the salt. Grease the dough with oil and let rise for 45 minutes in a bowl covered with plastic wrap. Remove the plastic wrap, punch down the dough with a closed fist, and let rise for another 20 minutes.
3. Turn the dough out onto the floured work surface. Give the dough two turns, shaping it into a long loaf. Arrange it on a lightly greased sheet of parchment paper placed in a basket lined with a cloth. Cover and let rise for half an hour.
4. Gently lift the ends of the parchment paper and transfer the loaf to a baking sheet. Make a series of parallel slashes on the surface of the dough and bake at 425°F (220°C) for 20 minutes.

Ingredients for 12 small loaves:

2 tsp (10 g) fresh yeast or 1⅔ tsp (5 g) dry yeast

1 cup + 2¼ oz (300 mL) lukewarm water

1⅓ Tbsp (20 g) extra-virgin olive oil

3¾ cups (450 g) all-purpose flour

1 Tbsp (18 g) salt

Pita Greece

Of Turkish origin, pita is now a typical Greek bread and is served with classic garlic, cucumber, fish, and eggplant dips. It's popular throughout the Middle East.

Preparation time: 30 minutes, plus 2 hours for rising. *Baking time:* 5 minutes.

1. Crumble the yeast in a large bowl, steadily pour in the lukewarm water, and mix with a wooden spoon. Add the olive oil and then a handful of flour. Continue to mix. When the mixture is well-blended, cover the bowl and let rest for 5 minutes. Then add the rest of the flour and the salt and knead vigorously on the floured work surface until the dough is shiny, firm, and elastic. Grease uniformly with oil, gently place in a bowl, cover with a damp dishcloth, and let rise for 1½ hours.

2. Turn the dough out onto the work surface and divide it into 12 equal portions. Shape these into 12 small balls and arrange them, well-spaced, on a floured baking sheet. Cover with a lightly dampened cloth and let rise for 10 minutes.

3. With a floured rolling pin, roll into 12 circles, each ¼ inch (5 mm) thick. Place them on a lightly floured cloth, away from drafts, and let rise for 30 minutes.

4. Grease several baking sheets, put the empty sheets in the oven, and bring the temperature to 480°F (250°C). With the help of an oven mitt, arrange the pitas on the hot baking sheets and let them bake for 5 minutes.

5. Afterwards, transfer the pita to a wire rack and let cool.

Ingredients for 15 small breads:

8¾ cups (1 kg) bread flour

4 tsp (20 g) fresh yeast

2¼ tsp (15 g) malt extract or 3¾ tsp (15 g) sugar

1 cup + 6½ oz (550 g) water

1 Tbsp (18 g) salt

extra-virgin olive oil

Arabic bread Arabia

Very soft and lightly baked, this bread lends itself to being stuffed. It goes well with soft cheeses, fish soups, and stewed meats.

Preparation time: 15 minutes, plus 1½ hours for rising. *Baking time:* 15 minutes.

1. Pour the flour onto the work surface, make a well in the center, and in the middle of the well dissolve the crumbled yeast and malt extract in a little water. Continue to blend in the flour a little at a time, adding water as needed, and then add the salt. The dough should be rather soft. Knead well for about 15 minutes, slamming down the dough repeatedly (see p. 17); use a dough cutter if the dough is very soft. Shape into a ball and place in a well-greased bowl; cover with a floured cloth and let rise for 30 minutes.
2. Turn the dough out onto the work surface and divide it into about 15 small balls that you place directly, well-spaced, on a baking sheet that is already lined with parchment paper. Sprinkle the balls with flour and cover them with another sheet of dampened parchment paper. Let rise for 20 minutes.
3. Flatten out the balls with the palm of your hand. They must be very flat. Let them rise for another 20 minutes and bake at about 480°F (250°C) for 15 minutes. Let cool on a wire rack.

Ingredients for 10 tortillas:

5 cups + 3⅓ oz (650 g) all-purpose flour

2¼ tsp (7 g) dry yeast or 5 tsp (25 g) fresh yeast

½ tsp (3 g) salt

2 Tbsp (30 g) margarine

1 cup + 1⅔ oz (370 g) hot water

cooking oil

Tortillas <small>Mexico</small>

In Mexico and Latin America, tortillas aren't only small breads but also serve as forks, knives, and plates. Tortillas may be wide and flat or small and thick, depending on the region and family traditions. They go well with flavorful foods, sauces, and salsas.

Preparation time: 20 minutes. *Cooking time:* 20 minutes.

1. Mix the flour, yeast, and salt in a bowl. Add the margarine, which has been cut into small pieces, and mix all the ingredients together while steadily and slowly pouring the hot water into the bowl. You may not need to use all of the water; you can add more water during kneading. Transfer the dough to a floured work surface and knead for about 10 minutes—until the dough is elastic and compact. Place in a well-greased bowl, cover, and let sit for 10 minutes.

2. Turn the dough out onto the work surface and divide it into 10 small, equal-sized balls. Roll these out with a rolling pin to a thickness of ¼ inch (5 mm) each.

3. Heat a cast iron skillet and when it is hot, cook the tortillas about 1 minute on each side. Serve warm, wrapped in a napkin.

Ingredients for 8 chapati:

2 cups + 4 tsp (250 g) all-purpose flour

about 1 cup (240 mL) water

1 tsp (6 g) salt

3⅓ to 4¼ oz (100 to 125 mL) ghee* or melted butter

*Ghee, clarified butter, can be found in grocery stores specializing in Indian foods, or you can make your own.

Chapati and paratha India

These are yeastless breads that accompany seasoned and very spicy foods. They need to be cooked on a hot skillet, such as a heavy cast-iron skillet.

Preparation time: 30 minutes. *Cooking time:* 1½ minutes.

1. Put 2 cups + 4 teaspoons (250 g) of flour into a bowl and slowly add 1⅔ ounces (50 mL) of water. Mix quickly and add another 1⅔ ounces (50 mL) of water. While you are mixing with your fingertips, steadily pour in enough water to make a very sticky dough. Knead for awhile without flouring your hands and then add the salt. When the dough becomes firm and elastic, but is still a little sticky, cover with a damp cloth and let rest for 5 to 10 minutes. Flour your hands and work surface well. Take a small amount of the dough at a time from the bowl and shape it into small balls each the size of an egg. Roll them out to ⅛ inch (3 mm) thick with a floured rolling pin. Dip rolling pin in dry flour to keep from sticking.

2. Heat an iron skillet without greasing it. Place the chapati in the skillet and cook 30 seconds on each side. Turn with tongs, and press down on the chapati with a folded cloth to cook it uniformly. Place the chapati on absorbent paper and brush with ghee or melted butter. Serve immediately.

3. Paratha are actually elaborate chapati that are made by first folding the dough and then rolling it out many times with a rolling pin. Cook the paratha 30 seconds on each side, brushing first with ghee or melted butter. Serve immediately.

Ingredients for 10 naan:

2 cups + 4 tsp (250 g) flour

1 tsp (6 g) salt

1 tsp (4.5 g) baking soda

1 tsp (4.5 g) cream of tartar

2 Tbsp (30 mL) plain yogurt

about 3¾ oz (110 mL) lukewarm water

cumin (optional)

coriander (optional)

sesame (optional)

Naan India

Naan is usually baked in a clay oven called a tandoor, which uses coal or wood, but you can cook it on a baking sheet or a very hot oven rack. Flavor with cumin, coriander, and sesame.

Preparation time: 15 minutes. *Baking time:* 1 minute.

1. Preheat the oven broiler to the highest temperature. In a bowl, mix the flour with the salt, baking soda, and cream of tartar. Make a well in the center and add the yogurt.

2. Steadily pour in the lukewarm water and begin to mix the dough with your fingertips; add water until it is soft and a little sticky. With a wooden spoon, mix the dough vigorously for one minute.

3. With well-floured hands, shape the dough into 10 small balls, each the size of an egg and roll them out with a rolling pin on a floured work surface. The rolled-out breads should each have a diameter of 6 inches (15 cm) and a thickness of about ⅜ inch (8 mm).

4. For a more exotic taste, before baking sprinkle the surface of the naan with coriander, cumin, and sesame seeds.

5. Place the naan on a hot baking sheet and bake under the broiler for 30 seconds on each side. Serve immediately.

Ingredients for 2 challah:

7¾ cups (930 g) all-purpose flour

6⅔ tsp (20 g) dry yeast or 14 tsp (70 g) fresh yeast

1¾ tsp (11 g) salt

10 Tbsp (120 g) sugar or 6 Tbsp (120 g) honey

1 cup + 5⅔ oz (400 mL) lukewarm water

4 lightly beaten eggs

8⅔ Tbsp (120 g) cooled melted butter

extra-virgin olive oil

To finish:

1 egg beaten with a little milk

poppy or sesame seeds

Challah Israel

Challah is bread for the celebration of the Jewish sabbath. It can be made in the shape of a braid or a spiral. Flavorful, rich, and slightly sweet, it is ideal for eating with butter and jam.

Preparation time: 30 minutes, plus 2 hours for rising. *Baking time:* 40 minutes.

1. In a bowl, sift 2 cups (260 g) of flour, add the yeast, salt, and sugar and mix well.

2. Make a well in the center of the dry ingredients. Beat the mixture with a whisk or a wooden spoon as you steadily pour in the warm water. Then add the lightly beaten eggs and the butter. Continue to beat vigorously with the whisk for about 3 minutes, gradually adding the rest of the flour. Use the whisk as long as possible; then turn the dough out onto a floured work surface.

3. Knead the dough for awhile, adding several tablespoons of flour if necessary, because the dough must be elastic yet somewhat firm. Grease with oil and let rise for one hour in a bowl covered with plastic wrap.

4. Punch down the dough with a closed fist and transfer it to a lightly floured work surface. Divide it in two equal parts and shape each part into a thick log and then wrap it snailwise around itself (see photo).

5. Cover and let rise for 40 minutes. To finish, lightly beat the egg with the milk and brush it on the two loaves. Then sprinkle a handful of poppy or sesame seeds over the surface of the dough. Bake for 40 minutes in an oven preheated to 355°F (180°C).

6. When the loaves are nicely golden, remove them from the baking sheet using a long spatula so they don't break, and let cool on a wire rack. Before cutting the loaves, be sure that they have cooled.

Ingredients for 12 breads:

4 cups + 1⅓ oz (500 g) all-purpose flour

2 Tbsp (30 g) fresh yeast or 2½ tsp (8 g) dry yeast

1 tsp (4 g) sugar

1 cup + 2¼ oz (300 mL) lukewarm water

3½ tsp (20 g) salt

2 Tbsp (28 g) extra-virgin olive oil

To finish (optional):

sesame or caraway seeds

olive oil

water

Barbari Iran

Preparation time: 20 minutes, plus 1½ hours for rising. *Baking time:* 30 minutes.

1. Sift the flour in a bowl and make a well in the center. Dissolve the yeast and sugar in the water and pour this into the center of the well. Mix with your fingertips, adding only a little flour until you make a creamy mixture.

2. Cover the bowl with plastic wrap and let dough rise for about 15 minutes. Remove the plastic wrap, mix in the remaining flour and the salt, and knead until the dough is well-blended. The dough should not be sticky.

3. In a second bowl, pour in the 2 tablespoons (28 g) of oil and place the dough in the bowl in order to grease it uniformly. Re-cover with the plastic wrap and let rise for 40 minutes.

4. Transfer the dough to the work surface, divide it into 12 portions, and shape into small oval breads. Flatten out the breads and slash with two diagonal, parallel cuts. Grease with a little oil, cover with a cloth, and let rise for 30 minutes. Bake in an oven preheated to 425°F (220°C) for 20 to 30 minutes or, if you wish, halfway through the baking, brush the surface of the breads with water and oil and sprinkle a handful of sesame or caraway seeds on them.

Decorative breads

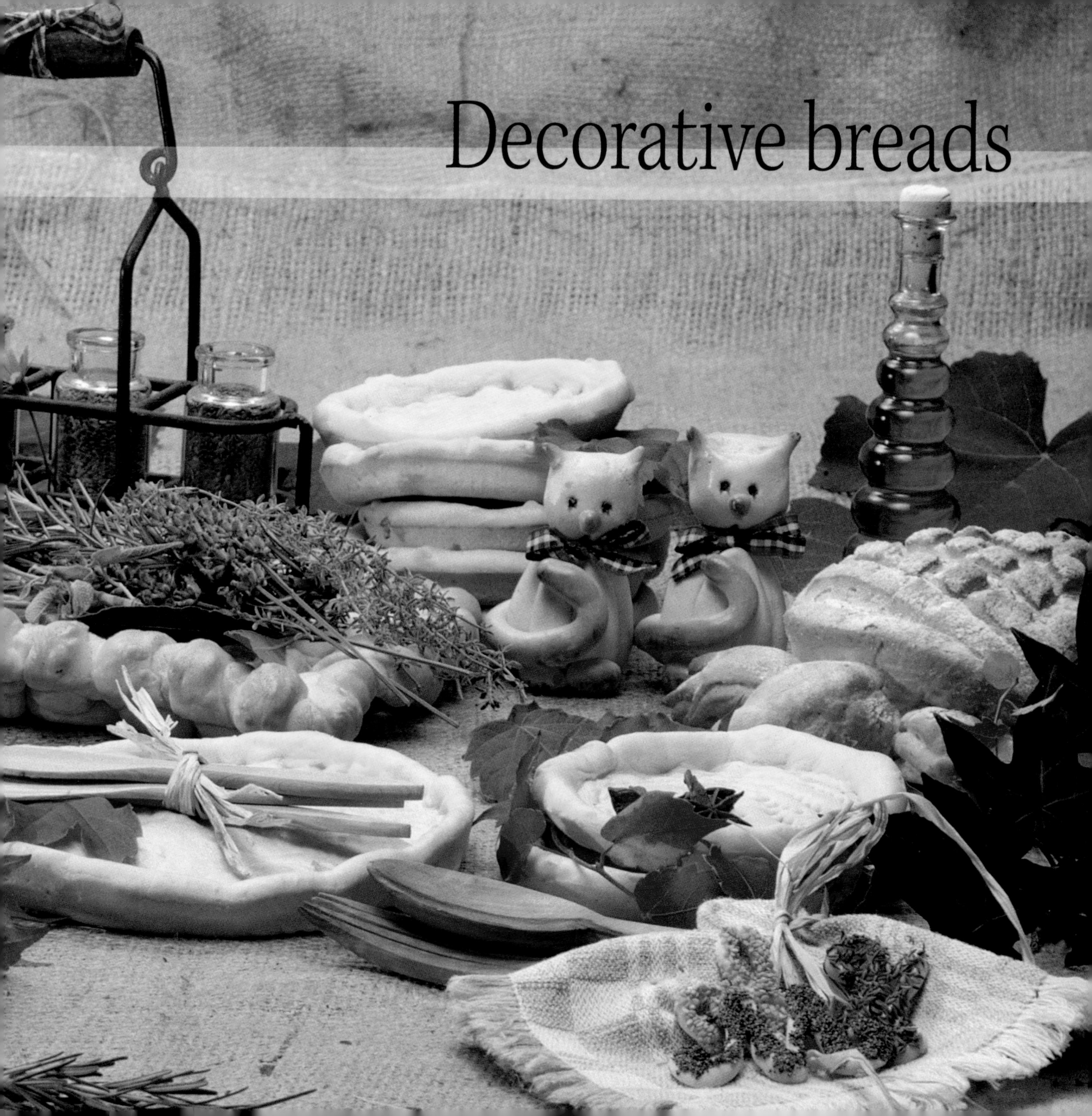

Ingredients: for 1 large sun or for 2 small suns:

11¾ cups (1600 g) all-purpose flour

3⅓ Tbsp (50 g) fresh yeast

1 Tbsp (20 g) malt extract or 2½ tsp (10 g) sugar

4¼ cups (1 L) water

2⅔ Tbsp (50 g) salt

extra-virgin olive oil

Suns

If you are mixing and kneading by hand, prepare the dough in two batches, because it is not easy to handle dough of this quantity.

Preparation time: 1 hour, plus 1 hour for rising. *Baking time:* 20 to 30 minutes.

1. Sift the flour onto the work surface, make a well in the center, crumble the yeast into the middle of the well, add the malt extract, then steadily pour in the water. Begin to mix with your fingertips. When the dough starts to come together, add the salt. Knead for about 15 minutes until the dough is soft, compact, and elastic. Grease the dough uniformly with oil, transfer it to a large bowl, cover with plastic wrap, and let rise for 20 minutes.

2. Remove the plastic wrap and transfer the dough to a floured work surface. With the dough cutter, divide the dough into many small pieces, which will be the sun's rays, and shape them into ropes.

3. Take one section of the dough and shape it into a small spiral, for the center of the sun. Shape the dough ropes with your hands into the form of sun rays, twisting the dough on itself several times. Do the same with the other ropes until you finish the sun.

4. Dust with flour, cover with a cloth, and let rise for 30 to 40 minutes away from drafts. Bake in an oven preheated to 425°F (220°C) for about half an hour. Let cool on the same baking sheet.

Cats

Ingredients: for 4 cats:
1½ cups (180 g) flour
1⅔ oz (50 mL) milk
1 egg yolk
2 Tbsp (28 g) extra-virgin olive oil
whole cloves

For the glaze:
1 egg
2 Tbsp (30 mL) milk
a pinch salt

Preparation time: 40 minutes. *Baking time:* 30 minutes.

1. Sift the flour onto the work surface, make a well in the center, and add in the mixed-together milk, egg yolk, and oil. Mix and knead until the dough is soft, elastic, and somewhat firm. With part of the dough, make the body of the cat, which should be the size of an egg. Flatten out the dough and put a toothpick in the center lengthwise with the top part of the toothpick sticking out of the neck.

2. Front legs: Shape a little ball the size of a small egg, flatten, and make one end into a point. With a knife, put a line down the middle. Back legs: Make two small balls with small lines for toes. Head: Make a larger ball and pinch the top to make the ears.

3. Attach the head to the toothpick sticking out of the top, insert cloves for eyes, and add a small ball of dough for the nose. Attach the legs, wetting the body of the cat with a little water. Make a dough rope for the tail and attach it. Make 3 more cats the same way.

4. Prepare the glaze by beating the egg with the milk and salt. Brush on the cats. Bake in 355°F (180°C) oven for about 30 minutes.

Ingredients for 2 turtles:

3⅓ cups (400 g) all-purpose flour

1 Tbsp (15 g) fresh yeast

¾ tsp (5 g) malt extract or 1¼ tsp (5 g) sugar

8½ oz (250 mL) water

2½ tsp (15 g) salt

extra-virgin olive oil

Turtle

These turtles might wander over to your table for a lawn party or picnic.

Preparation time: 1 hour, plus about 1 hour for rising. *Baking time:* 20 to 30 minutes.

1. Sift the flour onto the work surface, make a well in the center, and crumble the yeast into the center of the well. Add the malt extract and then steadily pour in the water. Begin to mix with your fingertips. When the dough has come together, add the salt. Knead for about 15 minutes until the dough is soft, compact, and elastic. Grease the dough uniformly with oil, transfer it to a large bowl, cover with plastic wrap, and let rise for 30 minutes.

2. Remove the plastic wrap and transfer the dough to a floured work surface. With a dough cutter, divide it into 4 sections. Shape two sections into small round loaves for the bodies of the turtles. Shape the other two sections into ropes and cut each into 6 pieces to make the head, feet, and tail.

3. Arrange the turtles on a baking sheet lined with parchment paper. With a sharp knife, create the shell design by making a series of crisscross cuts. Dampen the outside edge of the body of each turtle and attach the feet, tail, and head.

4. Dust the turtles with flour, cover with a cloth, and let rise for 30 to 40 minutes, away from drafts. Bake in an oven preheated to 425°F (220°C) for about half an hour. Let cool on the same baking sheet.

Ingredients for 1 large bunch of wheat:

11½ cups (1350 g) all-purpose flour

3⅓ tsp (20 g) salt

2 tsp (8 g) sugar

1 Tbsp (15 g) fresh yeast

3 cups (700 mL) luke-warm water

extra-virgin olive oil

water

For the glaze:

2 eggs

a pinch of salt

Harvest bread

Preparation time: 1 hour and 30 minutes. *Baking time:* 40 minutes.

1. In a large bowl, mix the flour, salt, and sugar. Make a well and crumble the yeast into the center of the well. Steadily pour in the water a little at a time, mix, and then knead. Grease the dough with oil, place on a baking sheet, cover with a lightly dampened cloth, and let rise for 1 hour.

2. Punch down the dough, knead, and divide into 7 balls. Take 1 (about 300 g). Cover the rest with a damp cloth. Roll out the ball of dough with a rolling pin, cut the dough into the shape of a mushroom, and bake in an oven preheated to 425°F (220°C) for 20 minutes.

3. For the stalks: prepare about 30 long, thin ropes from the dough and arrange on the base of the dough mushroom, which you have dampened with some water. For the wheat spikes: make small balls, giving them a typical tapered shape. Snip the surface of the balls with small scissors, wet the bottoms, and randomly attach to the dough mushroom. For the rope: braid three dough ropes. For the little mouse: make a point at one end of a little dough ball, make two cuts for the ears and two holes for the eyes. Attach a small rope of dough for the tail. Place the mouse on the base of the stalks. Prepare the glaze by beating the eggs with the salt. Brush it on the bread. With the tip of a knife, make a series of cuts lengthwise to make the stalks appear more natural. Bake at 390°F (200°C) for 15 minutes. Brush again with the glaze; reduce the temperature to 340°F (170°C) and bake for 25 minutes. Let cool on the baking sheet.

Ingredients for 5 small hedgehogs or 2 large ones:

2.2 pounds (1 kg) of bread dough made from all-purpose flour or whole wheat flour

1 Tbsp (15 mL) juniper berries

extra-virgin olive oil

Hedgehogs

These little hedgehogs make festive table decorations.

Preparation time: varies with recipe. *Baking time:* 15 minutes (small hedgehogs); 30 minutes (large hedgehogs).

1. Prepare the dough yourself by following any of the bread recipes.
2. Divide the dough into 2 equal portions for large hedgehogs or 5 equal portions for small hedgehogs. Take one and shape into an oval ball which is

slightly pointed on one end. Insert three juniper berries: two for the eyes and one for the nose.
3. With sharp, pointed scissors, snip the top of the ball to create the hedgehog's spiny hairs.
4. Cover with a dishcloth and let rise away from drafts for up to 15 minutes.
5. Place the hedgehogs on a baking sheet lined with a lightly greased sheet of parchment paper. Bake at 375°F (190°C); the small hedgehogs need to bake for about 15 minutes, the large ones for 30 minutes.

4 cups + 1⅓ oz (500 g) all-purpose flour

7½ Tbsp (106 g) extra-virgin olive oil

6⅔ to 8½ oz (200 to 250 mL) lukewarm water

1 tsp (5 g) fresh yeast

3¾ tsp (15 g) sugar or 1 tsp (7 g) malt extract

4 tsp (25 g) fine-grain salt

To finish:

1 egg, beaten

sesame or poppy seeds

Letters and hearts

Good for table decorations, napkin holders, or snacks.

Preparation time: 40 minutes, plus 40 minutes for rising. *Baking time:* 15 minutes.

1. Sift the flour onto the work surface, make a well in the center, and pour 3½ Tbsp (50 g) of oil and the water (in which the yeast has been dissolved) into the center of the well. Add the malt extract or sugar, begin to mix, and add the salt last.

2. Knead the dough for awhile so it becomes soft and elastic. Add 4 tablespoons (56 g) of extra-virgin olive oil to a large bowl, place the dough in the bowl, and turn it around so that it is uniformly greased with the oil. Cover with plastic wrap and let rise for half an hour.

3. Turn the dough out onto the work surface. Divide it with the dough scraper, first in half and then into many pieces of equal size to end up with 20 pieces.

4. Take one piece at a time and roll it between the palms of your hands to shape it into a breadstick. Then give it the desired shape: a letter, a heart, or other shape. To finish, brush the surface with the beaten egg and sprinkle with sesame or poppy seeds.

5. Repeat the same procedure with the other pieces of dough. Little by little, as they are ready, place the dough shapes neatly and well-spaced onto a baking sheet lined with parchment paper. Let rise for about 10 minutes. Bake at 390°F (200°C) for about 15 minutes.

Ingredients for 5 to 6 trays:

8⅓ cups (1 kg) all-purpose flour

1¾ oz (50 g) lard

3⅓ tsp (20 g) fine-grain salt

2½ Tbsp (50 g) malt extract

1 cup + 7⅓ oz (450 mL) ice water

extra-virgin olive oil

Trays

What a nice way to serve appetizers! It's not every day that you get to eat your dishes.

Preparation time: 1 hour. *Baking time:* 20 to 30 minutes.

1. Sift the flour onto the work surface, make a well, and in the center add the lard, salt, and the malt extract. Steadily pour in the water and begin to mix and knead vigorously. If necessary, add a little more water. This dough is difficult to knead.

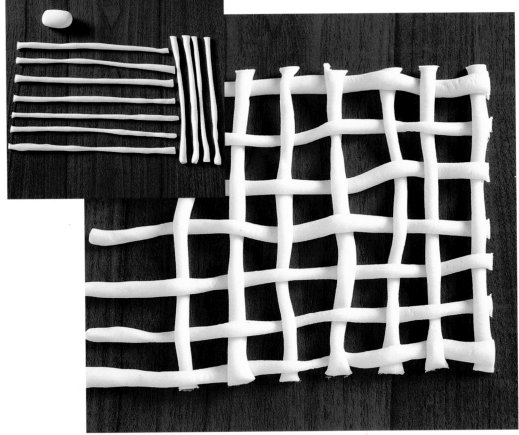

2. Divide the dough into many equal parts and then shape into ropes. Weave them into tray shapes on a baking sheet lined with parchment paper. Trim the edges with scissors or a sharp knife. Brush the trays with oil and bake at 355°F (180°C) for 20 to 30 minutes.

3. Let the bread trays cool before removing them from the baking sheet.

Ingredients for 5 to 6 plates:

8⅓ cups (1 kg) flour

1¾ oz (50 g) lard

3⅓ tsp (20 g) fine-grain salt

2½ Tbsp (50 g) malt extract

1½ cups (350 mL) ice water

extra-virgin olive oil

Plates and bowls

A festive way to serve food for a picnic, indoors or out.

Preparation time: 1 hour. *Baking time:* 30 to 40 minutes.

1. Sift the flour onto the work surface, make a well in the center, and add the lard, salt, and the malt extract. Steadily pour in the water and begin to mix and knead vigorously. If necessary, add a little more water, as the dough is hard to knead.

2. Grease the backs of ovenproof dishes or metal bowls with extra-virgin olive oil, cover them with the dough, and trim the overhanging edges with scissors or a sharp knife. Shape the dough to make an edge on each one. Make shallow edges for plates and deeper ones for bowls. Set on a greased baking sheet and bake everything for 30 to 40 minutes in an oven preheated to 355°F (180°C).

3. Let cool before removing the plates or bowls from the baking sheet.

Index